Advanced AI Techniques for Cybersecurity: Concepts, Architectures, and Emerging Trends

Rahul Karne

Sai Teja Erukude

Suhasnadh Reddy Veluru

Viswa Chaitanya Marella

notionpress.com

INDIA • SINGAPORE • MALAYSIA

ISBN
Paperback 979-8-90392-163-8
Hardcase 979-8-90392-164-5

Preface

The rapid evolution of digital technologies has fundamentally transformed the way societies operate, communicate, and innovate. Alongside these advancements, however, the cybersecurity threat landscape has grown increasingly complex, adaptive, and persistent. Traditional security mechanisms, while foundational, are no longer sufficient to counter sophisticated cyberattacks that leverage automation, scale, and intelligence. In this context, Artificial Intelligence (AI) has emerged as a powerful enabler, offering dynamic, data-driven, and predictive capabilities to strengthen cybersecurity defenses.

This book, ***Advanced AI Techniques for Cybersecurity: Concepts, Architectures, and Emerging Trends,*** is conceived as a comprehensive resource that explores the intersection of AI and cybersecurity. It presents a systematic discussion of core concepts, modern architectures, and cutting-edge techniques such as machine learning, deep learning, neural networks, and intelligent automation as applied to threat detection, intrusion prevention, malware analysis, and cyber resilience. In addition, the book highlights emerging research trends, real-world applications, and future directions that are shaping the next generation of intelligent security systems.

The primary objective of this work is to bridge the gap between theoretical foundations and practical implementations. It is intended to serve a diverse audience including students, researchers, academicians, and industry professionals who seek to understand and apply advanced AI-driven approaches to cybersecurity challenges. By integrating conceptual clarity with applied insights, this book aims to contribute meaningfully to both academic research and professional practice in the domain.

We hope that this book inspires further exploration, innovation, and collaboration in the rapidly evolving field of AI-enabled cybersecurity.

Dedication

This book is dedicated to our families. Thank you for your patience, understanding, and unconditional support throughout the many months of planning, writing, revising, and refining. You stood by us during late nights and busy weekends, encouraged us when the workload felt heavy, and reminded us to keep moving forward. Your belief gave us the confidence to stay committed to this goal, and your support made this book possible in ways that go beyond words.

We also dedicate this work to the learners who are building their path in cybersecurity and applied AI. If you are a student, a professional transitioning into security, or someone trying to keep up with fast-changing threats and technologies, this book is for you. We wrote it to make advanced ideas more approachable, to connect theory with practical thinking, and to encourage careful, responsible use of emerging techniques. Security is not only about tools or alerts. It is about mindset, clarity, and making decisions that reduce risk and protect people.

Finally, we dedicate this book to everyone working to make the digital world safer. The work is often challenging and invisible, but it matters deeply. We hope this book contributes to stronger defenses, better understanding, and a culture of ethical innovation and continuous learning.

Acknowledgement

The completion of this book would not have been possible without the support, guidance, and contributions of many individuals and institutions. We would like to express our sincere gratitude to our mentors and academic guides for their invaluable insights, constructive feedback, and continuous motivation throughout the development of this work.

We are thankful to our colleagues and peers for engaging discussions, technical inputs, and encouragement that helped refine the ideas presented in this book. Their perspectives and collaborative spirit significantly enriched the quality of the content.

We also acknowledge the support of our respective institutions for providing a conducive academic environment and access to resources essential for research and writing. Special thanks are extended to the publishers and editorial team for their professional assistance, patience, and guidance during the publication process.

Above all, we express our heartfelt appreciation to our families for their unwavering support, understanding, and inspiration, which made it possible for us to pursue and complete this endeavor.

Contents

Chapter 1

Foundations of AI in Cybersecurity

1.1 Overview of AI and Machine Learning in Security

One of the significant factors that is dramatically transforming the cybersecurity industry is the adoption of Artificial Intelligence (AI) and Machine Learning (ML) as they enable companies to implement preventive, adaptive security measures instead of the traditional reactive ones. Moreover, the traditional security methods that depend on fixed rules and known threat profiles usually struggle to cope with the modern hackers' actions which are not only more advanced but also greater in number, such as polymorphic malware and zero-day exploits. The mentioned issues are being addressed by AI and ML through the provision of the systems with the ability to analyze extensive amounts of data in real time, to recognize complex patterns, to detect anomalies, and to reveal even the slightest compromise indicators which would be extremely difficult for human analysts to find by their own efforts. The aforementioned circumstances where the threat detection is fast and accurate, the vulnerability detection is done in a proactive way, and routine tasks like network log analysis and initial incident response which are traditionally tedious and labor-intensive, are automated thus greatly decreasing response times and cutting down possible damages from successful attacks. Humans will continue to be trained and supported by AI, thus their skills will be transferred to areas that are more intricate and where human intuition and creative problem-solving are needed.

1.1.1 AI in Security

AI's contribution to the advancement in detection and response capabilities is viewed as one of the primary benefits of its utilization in the security sector. AI technologies can help organizations cope with cyberattacks and data leaks more efficiently, as they will already support the automation of threat detection, prevention, and remediation (Shrivastav et al., 2025).

Organizations can integrate AI into cybersecurity in numerous ways. A majority of the AI-powered security solutions rely on machine learning (ML) and deep learning (DL) technologies which are able to the throughput and processing of huge volumes of information which encompass, but are not limited to, the data concerning users' internet activity, patterns of application usage, and navigation habits on the internet as well as other data connected to network activity.

AI is able to identify trends and provide a security baseline thanks to this analysis. Any action that deviates from the baseline is promptly identified as an anomaly and possible cyberthreat, enabling prompt correction.

Additionally, generative AI (gen AI), made popular by large language models (LLMs), is often used by AI security systems to transform security data into suggestions in plain English, simplifying decision-making for security teams.

AI security solutions greatly enhance threat detection and incident response, according to research. Organizations with full security AI and automation were able to identify and contain data breaches 108 days faster on average than those without AI solutions, according to the IBM Cost of a Data Breach Report.

1.1.2 Why AI Security is Important

Depending on the situation, AI security can mean many things. Although the use of AI to enhance cybersecurity is the main topic of this site, two additional frequent definitions focus on protecting AI models and algorithms against unauthorized access or harmful usage.

According to one definition, cybersecurity specialists concentrate on how threat actors are utilizing AI to enhance their cyberattacks or take advantage of fresh assault opportunities.

According to research, threat detection and incident response are greatly enhanced by AI security systems. Businesses with full security AI and automation were able to identify and contain data breaches 108 days faster on average than those without AI solutions, according to the IBM Cost of a Data Breach Report.

LLMs, for example, can assist attackers in crafting more complex and individualized phishing assaults. Because AI models are a relatively new technology, they also give threat actors new ways to launch cyberattacks, including adversarial and supply chain attacks (see "Potential vulnerabilities and security risks of AI").

The current state of cyberthreats is complicated. Data sprawl and increased attack surfaces have resulted from the move to cloud and hybrid cloud systems, and threat actors are always coming up with new ways to take advantage of weaknesses. With more than 700,000 job openings in the US alone, cybersecurity specialists are still in short supply.

As a result, cyberattacks are increasingly more common and expensive. The average cost of fixing a data breach worldwide in 2023 was USD 4.45 million, a 15% rise over three years, according to the Cost of a Data Breach Report.

AI security can be a remedy. AI, through automating the detection and response to threats, prevents attacks easily and also helps at the same time to recognize the attackers during the process. AI instruments can assist in all phases of getting rid of the malware by spotting and cutting off the bad software from the good one, to recognizing and stopping the repeated log-in attempts that are the signs of brute-force attacks being conducted.

1.1.3 Benefits of AI security

The utilization of AI technology can result in numerous advantages in the area of cybersecurity, thereby enhancing the overall defense system. AI security gives rise to a number of benefits, among which the following are the most noteworthy:

- **Enhanced threat detection**: AI algorithms process huge volumes of data instantaneously which results in faster and more precise identification of possible cyber threats. AI instruments are also capable of spotting complex ways of attacking that classic security systems might not be aware of.
- **Faster incident response**: The inclusion of AI in the cybersecurity field can greatly reduce the time required for the whole process of detection, investigation, and responding to security breaches. This way, the organizations will be able to face the threats sooner and the impact on them will be less.
- **Greater operational efficiency**: The manual tasks which AI tools can perform, therefore, making security operations easier and less costly. Moreover, by doing away with the human element in cybersecurity operations, the map of the security team's resources could be redrawn to incorporate more tactical projects.
- **Automated regulatory compliance**: The application of AI can facilitate compliance monitoring, data protection, and reporting by way of automation, thus ensuring that the companies met the regulatory requirements all the time.
- **Understanding emerging threats**: Utilizing AI in security measures gives businesses the advantage of always being one step ahead of the attackers. Machine learning, combined with the rapid data influx, equips the AI systems with the skill to recognize the emerging risks, and this is true for the case of guarding the cybernetworks against the new types of break-ins as well.
- **A proactive approach to cybersecurity**: The use of AI in security gives firms the opportunity to carry out a proactive strategy in their cybersecurity activities. This is achieved through the analysis of past incidents, forecasting of future cyberthreats, and disclosure of network weaknesses.

- **Improved user experience**: AI can improve the security measures while still keeping a good user experience. One such example might be AI biometrics and analyzing user behavior as a couple of new authentication methods with high security and seamlessness for users.
- **Ability to scale**: The AI cybersecurity tools are capable of expanding in their protective measures to cover large and complicated IT environments. Besides, they can be made to work seamlessly with the current cybersecurity applications and infrastructures, for instance, security information and event management (SIEM) systems, thus boosting the network's real-time threat intelligence and automated response capabilities.

1.1.4 Machine Learning in Security

Computers may learn without explicit programming thanks to machine learning (ML). In other words, machine learning teaches machines to learn via experience, much like humans do. One area of artificial intelligence is machine learning.

In the field of security, machine learning continuously learns by analyzing data to identify patterns. This makes it possible for us to more precisely identify internal threats, identify malware in encrypted communications, anticipate the locations of "bad neighborhoods" online to safeguard people while they browse, or safeguard data in the cloud by observing questionable user behavior.

How does machine learning work in security?

Organizations must continuously monitor and correlate millions of internal and external data points across their infrastructure and users due to the cyber threat environment. This amount of data just cannot be handled by a team of employees alone.

Machine learning excels in this situation because it can swiftly identify trends and anticipate dangers in enormous data sets. Cyber teams can quickly spot risks and circumstances that require more in-depth human investigation by automating the analysis.

How does ML work?

Let's review some important words because non-data scientists may find the specifics of machine learning perplexing.

Sets of training data, also referred to as "ground truth," which are exact question-and-answer pairs, are used in supervised learning. This training aids in the precise classification of data by classifiers, which are the cornerstones of machine learning analysis. Additionally, it facilitates the successful analysis of fresh data in the actual world by algorithms that are used to arrange and orient classifiers. Identifying faces in internet photographs is a common example: To accurately recognize a distinct face from millions of internet photographs, classifiers examine the data patterns they are trained on rather than the actual noses or eyes.

1.1.5 How machine learning helps security

1. **Find threats on a network:** By continuously observing network activity for irregularities, machine learning identifies dangers. To identify significant situations, machine learning engines evaluate enormous volumes of data in almost real time. These methods make it possible to identify policy infractions, undiscovered malware, and insider risks.
2. **Keep people safe when browsing:** In order to keep users from visiting harmful websites, machine learning can identify "bad neighborhoods" on the internet. In order to automatically detect attack infrastructures setup for both present and future threats, machine learning monitors Internet behavior.
3. **Provide endpoint malware protection:** Algorithms are able to identify malware that has never been seen before that is attempting to operate on endpoints. Based on the characteristics and actions of existing malware, it detects new dangerous files and activities.
4. **Protect data in the cloud:** By examining suspicious cloud app login activity, identifying location-based abnormalities, and doing IP reputation research to find threats and dangers in cloud

applications and platforms, machine learning helps safeguard productivity.

5. **Detect malware in encrypted traffic:** By analyzing the data components of encrypted traffic in routine network monitoring, machine learning algorithms aid in the detection of malware in encrypted communications. In order to identify the risks that are hidden by encryption, machine learning approaches measure the bad patterns rather than decoding the communication.

1.2 Cyber Threat Landscape and Modern Attack Vectors

The constantly evolving ecosystem of cyberthreats, attack techniques, and attack routes directed at individuals, governments, and corporations is known as the threat landscape. The complexity of cybercrime has evolved to a great extent, reaching its peak by the involvement of different threat entities such as hackers, governments, and criminal organizations which were the main creators of it, and also the factors like the rise of cloud computing, IoT devices, and global supply chains that are interlinked all contributed to the scenario (Harris, 2023).

The modifications have broadened the attack surface, thereby permitting the attackers to select from among a larger number of vulnerabilities. Knowing the current threat landscape is indispensable for risk identification, tracking of the attackers' activities, and cornering security measures that will not only protect the organization but also make it invulnerable. The modern-day threat scenario can be interpreted as a significant rise in both existing and probable threats which are becoming more and more frequent and intricate. Digitalization and the political scenario have not just created a shift in the criminals' methods but also shifted the focus of their attacks to both the assets and the people.

In cybersecurity, an attack vector is a method for gaining unauthorized network access to start a cyberattack. After a data breach, cybercriminals might use attack vectors to exploit system vulnerabilities and get sensitive data, personally identifiable information (PII), and other critical information.

Since the average cost of a data loss is $4.35 million, planning ahead is essential to minimizing potential attack vectors and averting data breaches. Digital forensics and IP attribution can help clean up data breaches, but avoiding them is much more important.

The most popular attack vectors are malware, viruses, email attachments, webpages, pop-ups, instant chats, text messaging, and social engineering. However, when hackers attempt to exploit unpatched or zero-day vulnerabilities disclosed on CVE and the dark web, the number of cyber threats keeps rising since there is no one solution to halt every attack vector.

1.2.1 The Current Cyber Threat Landscape

The threat landscape changes each time a new event substantially modifies or affects the context of impacted entities.

Below are some examples of recent events that have contributed to the current danger landscape.

1. The COVID-19 Pandemic

In 2020, lockdowns began all throughout the world, and companies had to adapt by offering work-from-home (WFH) options. Remote working greatly increased the attack surfaces of enterprises.

When the Bring-Your-Own-Device (BYOD) policy was implemented, new attack avenues were created. Plans for safeguarding unmanaged endpoints, such laptops and smartphones, must be developed by security specialists. Data breaches in the healthcare industry increased by 35% between 2020 and 2021 as a result of malicious actors swiftly exploiting the vulnerabilities.

2. The Russia-Ukraine Conflict

The situation with both countries has slowly developed and finally resulted in war. The Sophisticated cyber-attacks that Russia is known for have led to the speculation of its involvement in a series of worldwide attacks in 2022.

3. The Growing Adoption of Third-Party Vendors

The continuous increase in outsourcing of significant operations has been a major factor in the rise of third-party data breaches. Cybercriminals have taken advantage of this situation and are now focusing on supply chain attacks on a large scale. Hackers can access more sensitive data with less effort by concentrating on multiple third-party and fourth-party suppliers in a single assault.

1.2.2 Protection Against the Threat Landscape

To stay safe from the threat landscape, the organizations need to consider cybersecurity in a broad way. They have to take a proactive approach which involves not only threat mitigation but also lessening the susceptibility of their systems.

- **Recognize and Categorize Cyber Threats**

  Risk assessments need to be comprehensive and extensive in order for the specific cyber threats that are likely to affect your company to be identified. Understanding the modes of attack of ransomware, phishing, and APTs is the first step in developing defenses against them. Not only does this understanding of the threats help in the prioritization of resource allocation according to the urgency of the situation, it also helps the security personnel to concentrate their efforts on the parts of the security perimeters that are the weakest and therefore the most probable targets for attack.

  The companies that acquire knowledge about the tactics, techniques, and procedures (TTPs) of the adversaries will have the upper hand in mapping the potential routes of attacks and consequently will be able to implement more effective security controls.

- **Deepen Visibility Across Your Attack Surface**

  Being aware of your attack surface is very important since it shows the areas where a malicious person can exploit the vulnerabilities. Regular surveillance and mapping out of the company's digital assets will help in detecting the possible entry points for attacks. The whole procedure requires looking into the cloud, IoT, endpoint, and even connecting third parties—these are typically the places that have hidden flaws.

The firms can detect their weak points in the defense line, monitor the situation in real-time, and take precautions to prevent the cyber threat from escalating a major issue just by guaranteeing visibility. With such a strict attitude towards the attack surface, one can see where the repairs need to be done and thus the risk of encountering security breaches is significantly lowered.

- **Deploy Effective Defensive Strategies**

  Defensive strategies are a crucial matter mitigating the towering threats that cannot be alienated:

  - **Make Use of MDR or SCDR Services:** Aided by advanced machine learning algorithms, Supply Chain Detection and Response (SCDR) and Managed Detection and Response (MDR) can swiftly detect threats and monitor in real time.
  - **Adopt a Cyber Resilience Strategy:** In case of threats with respect to data security, the best defense is to have a plan set in place that promptly brings desired actions.
  - **Cybersecurity Policies Should Be Kept Up-To-Date:** An organization that has updated policies and procedures is ready to resist new attack techniques.
  - **Employee Cybersecurity Training Must Be the Top Priority:** The training program should incorporate the aspect of recognizing and thwarting potential social engineering attacks, phishing schemes, and questionable activities. The training program should cover ways of recognizing and handling social engineering, phishing, and suspicious activities.

1.2.3 Types of Cyber Threats in the Threat Landscape

Each one of the cybersecurity hacks has more and more functionalities, for example, here are some techniques that can be used against an organization:

1. **Ransomware and Malware:** Ransomware continues to be the most destructive cybercrime by stealing and holding data at the same time. This malware is always changing its form, exploiting vulnerabilities in the operating system, cloud, and IoT devices. In addition, some ransomware groups apply double extortion strategies, threatening to make public the data they have stolen if their demands are not met.

2. **Social Engineering Attacks:** Social engineering attacks are methods of tricking individuals to unknowingly give away their account or information access. The easiest and widest spread of these techniques are phishing, pretexting, and baiting, and they all rely on human errors and cause security breaches. Such attacks are extremely damaging since they bypass the security measures entirely and exploit the trust factor within the organization.

3. **Data Breaches and Data Leaks:** The issue of unauthorized access to sensitive data is increasingly worrying. Malicious individuals take advantage of compromised credentials and unprotected systems to illegally access data. They take advantage of bad password practices, making secret data available. The impact of a breach usually leads to organizations incurring large expenditures for damage control and compliance measures.

4. **Denial of Service (DoS) and Distributed Denial of Service (DDoS):** The attack techniques mentioned here are a huge burden on the systems causing them to crash. Such methods frequently target main websites or services. The financial and reputation damage caused by DDoS attacks is being increasingly classified as a weapon. A lot of the attackers are now using

botnets to create stronger disruptions which in turn makes them harder to block.

5. **Advanced Persistent Threats (APTs):** Threats that are constant like APTs are the attacks that last for a long time and are directed at a specific target and usually perpetrated by countries or groups that have good funding. They take advantage of stealthy attack vectors to get into networks and steal sensitive information. APTs usually consist of several stages such as reconnaissance, initial compromise, and sustained access that are needed to achieve their objectives.
6. **Zero-Day Exploits:** Zero-day exploits are those vulnerabilities in software, hardware, or firmware that are not known to the respective vendors. They are still unpatched and very liable to be attacked. The attackers take advantage of these vulnerabilities to access systems and cause damages that may go undetected for a long time or result in a data breach, especially if the affected area has not yet been fixed.
7. **AI-Driven Cyber Attacks:** Malicious users are employing AI in order to automate and magnify their attack methods. Among these are AI-powered phishing campaigns and malware that adapts to the measures used for defense and are thus automatically generated. All of this makes it harder to actually detect and suppress those threats.

1.3 Data, Features, and Patterns in Security Analytics

Security analytics has been a prominent and very necessary aspect of cybersecurity and has been a great support in the shielding from cyber threats through its main function of scanning and identifying them beforehand. The analysis of the vast data collected from the digital footprint of the company is the technique which is being used for the detection and the one of the most common the application of the method is looking for any unusual activity as the pointer to the potential threat. The main focus is laid on the acquisition of the largest raw data amount possible which includes such basic inputs as system logs, network traffic metadata (NetFlow or IPFIX records), endpoint activity data (process execution, file changes), authentication logs, and threat intelligence feeds. The volume and diversity of the data require the use of powerful platforms, such as Security Information and Event Management (SIEM), which can handle processing, ingestion, and storage of the data in an efficient way to make it available for future analysis.

After gathering the information, the security analytics is concerned with the extraction of meaningful features and trends which can be used to detect some latent threats. Characteristics are derived attributes of the data, such as how often a particular user logs in, the amount of data exiting a network segment or the score of a reputation of a destination IP address. These characteristics are then broken down on the basis of statistical models, machine learning algorithms and pre-defined rules to detect patterns that do not conform to existing baselines of normal behavior.

1.3.1 Security Analytics

Organizations may obtain comprehensive insights into their security posture and any threats by utilizing security analytics solutions.

Security analytics systems continuously ingest data from events and alerts across the network (such as endpoint and user behavior data, operating system event logs, applications, network traffic analyzers, firewalls, routers, virus scanners, threat intelligence feeds, and contextual data) in order to detect and respond to incidents in real time.

If properly set, this information is evaluated to proactively detect breaches by searching for abnormalities like malware, ransomware, strange traffic, or unusual application activity. This can reduce the false positive rate compared to relying on isolated events from a single security control.

For precise security posture monitoring, security analytics tools measure corporate risk and rank risk reduction initiatives. They take in and examine information from cloud environments, vulnerability scans, software bill of materials (SBOM), asset inventories, configuration management databases (CMDBs), and other pertinent IT and security technologies.

1.3.2 AI and Machine Learning for Security Analytics

The sheer amount of data generated by any particular environment may include information about suspicious events that security personnel should look at but are difficult to locate by hand. It becomes futile to have SecOps do repetitious tasks around-the-clock, because consistency and continuity cannot be guaranteed.

The most effective solution to the problem of repetitive tasks for teams is to implement AI and ML. They can reduce the fatigue and burnout of security teams, guarantee better consistency all the time and even release time for the development of an organization's security position.

In the case of security, they may enable the related teams to spot a cyber-attack beforehand with a considerably lower False Positive rate and thus acquire useful information for arresting coming threats. Likewise, sophisticated AI and ML techniques can assist companies in constructing integrated risk models capable of evaluating their cyber risk, foreseeing potential breach scenarios, estimating breach impact in dollars, and formulating action plans for both enhancing their security level and thwarting cyber-attacks.

1.3.3 Features of Security Analytics

The tools and functionality required to look into events, determine how IT systems are affected, and discover more about new threats are provided by security analytics. By providing extensive real-time visibility into an organization's present infrastructure, it increases security awareness.

Although no company can anticipate an impending danger, security analytics software allows businesses to anticipate the next assault and take the necessary precautions. They are able to close discovered security holes, address known and hidden vulnerabilities, and stay one step ahead of thieves.

IT teams are under tremendous pressure to inform stakeholders of their most recent discoveries. Security analytics tracks movement, maintains tabs on threat trends, and promptly notifies all corporate users when an abnormality is found.

Who uses Security Analytics?

Security analytics is used by almost all contemporary organizations with a digital presence or architecture. Teams of analysts, engineers, and other frontline personnel who employ security analytics make up Security Operations Centers (SOCs). Security analytics solutions are used by CISOs in organizations to ensure that sensitive data is adequately protected.

Businesses need security analytics because it enables them to identify dangers before they worsen, become serious problems, and result in data breaches. It is a preventive approach that ensures strong cyber security by adding an additional layer of protection.

13.4 Types of Security Analytics Tools

Here are the different types of security analytics tools you should know about:

- **Behavioral Analytics:** Behavioral analytics will examine the behavioral trends and patterns of users, apps, and devices. It will try to find abnormal behaviors, anomalies, and proof of anything that could indicate a potential security breach or incoming attack.

- **External Threat Intelligence:** Sometimes the threat intelligence generated by your organization isn't enough, which is when you resort to external threat intelligence as part of your security portfolio. These are specialized platforms that can support your analytical process.

- **Forensics Tools:** Forensics tools are used by every organization for evidence collection and to find out how attackers get into your organization and slip past defenses. They trace attack origins and can identify various security vulnerabilities and cyber threats. It can help you investigate ongoing incidents and also prevent system compromises.
- **Network Analysis and Visibility Tools:** These tools are used to analyze end-user and application traffic, including network flows. You can also call them network security monitoring solutions.
- **Security information and event management solutions (SIEM):** Solutions for event management and security information will assist you in analyzing security warnings in real time. They can also do log analysis and aggregate data that is generated by apps and network devices. You can also use SIEM solutions for real-time data streaming and to ingest data from any source to clean it up.

1.3.5 Patterns in Security Analytics

If you search for "Security Patterns" on Google, you'll discover that the phrase is used rather widely and that there are many differing views on what a pattern should stand for.

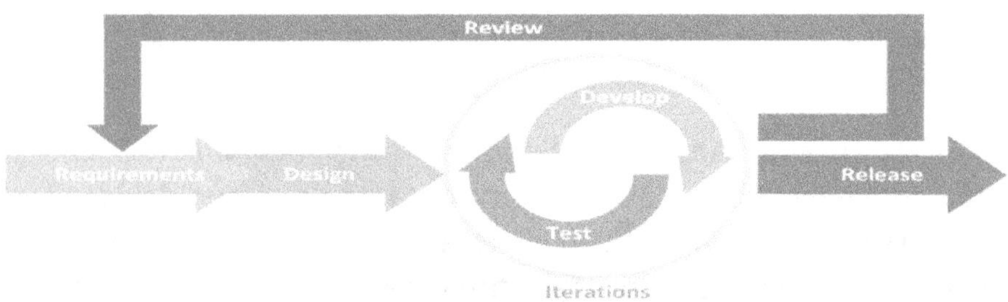

Figure 1.1: Security Pattern Flow

Source: (Security Patterns.io, 2024)

Since various designers will analyze issues at different levels, there is no "correct" amount of detail for what constitutes a security pattern. While the business security architecture could be more interested in trust connections between the organization and other parties, a security analyst might be more interested in patterns pertaining to particular software development.

All things considered, a security pattern is essentially a stated and reusable solution to a persistent security issue.

These include the security patterns listed below as design artifacts.

- Describes a security issue and how it impacts the asset.
- Derived from particular technology or vendor implementations.
- Promotes reusability by standardizing the use of taxonomies.
- Ensures that the dangers being mitigated may be linked to the required controls.

Why develop a security pattern?

The need for more intelligent approaches to security architecture and design is growing along with the information technology industry's demand and deployment speed. The industry is still pushing for quicker deployment cycles, although ten years ago they were scheduled around quarterly or monthly releases.

In order to stay up to date, any time and effort spent on creating security architecture and design must enable the development of artifacts that are reusable, flexible, and encourage knowledge exchange among peers.

1.4 Traditional vs AI-Driven Security Approaches

Static rule sets, attack signatures, and patterns are the primary means of threat identification and mitigation in traditional cybersecurity. The most popular tools in this category include intrusion detection and prevention systems (IDS/IPS), firewalls, antivirus software, malware sandboxes, and isolation. These solutions have limited effect on polymorphic malware or zero-day vulnerabilities, but they are extremely effective against established threats. Additionally, many of these solutions are seen as intrinsically reactive in an increasingly dynamic threat scenario since they need manual upgrades and setups.

AI-powered cybersecurity has the capability to predict and prevent advanced threats through the integration of technologies like machine learning (ML), hyperscale data analytics, and automation. Unlike the conventional systems, AI, through its real-time analysis, operates on enormous datasets, notices oddities, and even finds the most sophisticated types of attacks one of which is the zero-day exploit and the other is polymorphic malware. Moreover, the automatic way of detecting and responding to incidents decreases the need for human involvement, thus, making the threat control process quicker and more efficient.

For every business, security is the number one priority and it is very important to pick the right way of dealing with it. Anti-virus programs, firewalls, and human monitoring are some traditional security methods that have been in existence for a long time to provide protection for systems and data. Although these methods are efficient, they also have certain shortcomings especially when the cyber threats are developing and becoming more sophisticated.

On the other hand, artificial intelligence security measures are relying on AI or computer intelligence to boost protection. These contemporary techniques rely on machine learning and sophisticated algorithms for the detection and responding to threats much quicker than the old-fashioned way. AI security is capable of real-time adjustments to new threats, thus providing an upgraded protection level. Getting to know the disparities between the traditional and AI-assisted security techniques will allow us to take more intelligent steps toward system protection. Comparing the two techniques will provide a transparent perspective of their advantages and disadvantages which will help us select the most suitable one for our requirements. Let's investigate the specifics of these protective measures to reveal their capabilities in safeguarding our company.

1.4.1 Key Features of Traditional and AI Driven Approaches in Security:

Traditional:

- **Static detection models:** This is, therefore, dependent upon the pre-ordained threat signature or rule.

- **Basic protection:** Having the ability to combat previously identified risks and weaknesses, however, it does not work in the case of the attack that is absolutely novel and not seen before.
- **High maintenance needs:** Even with automated help, the process frequently involves a manual touch and/or a pair of eagle eyes looking out for what will make life simple.

AI Driven:

- **Advanced threat detection:** Uses anomaly detection and machine learning methods to find dangers that were previously unidentified.
- **Continuous adaptation:** Reduces false positives and negatives over time by learning from fresh data to keep ahead of the changing threat landscape.
- **Automation:** Automated incident response processes, threat intelligence production, and real-time detection.

1.4.2 AI vs. Traditional Cybersecurity in Action

- **Instant sensitive data classification:** Predictive AI and ML are the ones that automatically detect and categorize sensitive information from endpoints, inline traffic, and clouds. Thus, it is possible to apply protection more quickly and at the same time, traditional methods result in a significant reduction of breach risk.
- **AI-powered application segmentation:** The machine learning algorithms study the user log data and based on the user's conduct and the utilization of analogous applications; they suggest the particular parts of the application. The system-generated segments block lateral movement, decrease the attack surface, and lessen manual segmentation requirements.
- **AI-powered smart isolation:** The content of the web page is scanned in real-time, which consequently enables the immediate isolation of suspicious pages and the instant blocking of file and web threats that are coming up. The method offers

risk-free flexible policy execution and instant threat verdicts at the same time.

1.4.3 Benefits and Limitations of Traditional Security

Traditional security methods provide a variety of advantages that make them a dependable option for companies. A major benefit is their long-established record. Firewalls, antivirus programs, and IDS have been confirmed to be very effective in preventing attacks from well-known sources. They assure the security of the company's information to a certain extent and thus, become a part of the whole security strategy.

Another advantage is their simplicity of deployment and management. A lot of traditional security tools are easy to use, hence any company, regardless of size, can access them. Maintenance of their effectiveness by regular updates and patches, continuous protection against new threats is guaranteed.

Nevertheless, traditional security methods are not without their disadvantages. They mainly depend on signature-based detection which implies that they can only point out threats that have been previously documented. Thus, they are of little use in case of zero-day attacks—new and unknown threats that take advantage of the loopholes before they can be closed by updates.

Moreover, the old ways of handling the situations might not be fast enough to comprehend the ever-evolving and more sophisticated cyber threats. There are cases when Methods that are not modern might not be able to give complete security against the attackers who are professionally skillful. That is, companies may be exposed to advanced persistent threats (APTs) and the latest attack tactics thus losing their security.

1.5 Challenges in Applying AI to Cybersecurity

Artificial Intelligence, or in short AI, in the context of security measures implies the use of the smart robots' application, or in other words, the human-like computer programs, to strengthen the security rules. Primarily, the technologies that are being used are machine learning, neural networks, and data analytics, and they are all so powerful that they can automatically detect, respond to, and even prevent threats. Besides the usual data, AI would also be able to find the possible threats and incidents through data analysis, and still, it would be able to do so, along with the response actions, much quicker.

The application of machine learning algorithms has been the backbone in the recognition of patterns and anomalies which indicate potential security breaches over a long period of time, normally even before any serious damage occurs. Security systems with the application of this method have not only been able to cope with but also to counteract the new threats and attacks that are not included in the known patterns. The arrival of new technology like generative AI has greatly facilitated this whole process, and security systems are already capable of doing a comprehensive analysis of security data and suggesting the most optimal ways of minimizing vulnerabilities and mitigating threats.

1.5.1 Key Use Cases and Examples of AI in Cybersecurity

AI provides several capabilities for cybersecurity.

- **Endpoint Protection and Malware Detection**

  AI can undeniably play an enormous role in the functionality of security systems primarily in detecting and eliminating the malware. The drawbacks with signature-based detection methods are the inability to identify novel or evolving threats at times, which is worse when such threats do not even exist on the list. In contrast, the AI system employs machine learning models which are consistently updated with the skilful work over huge datasets to unveil the patterns that are similar to those of the malicious activities. The technique facilitates the identification of not only unknown dangers but also the non-requirement of any previous signatures and hence an overall more adaptable endpoint security system. The application of AI in all areas has quickened and improved the accuracy of malware analysis process. It can effectively and instantly filter a huge volume of security data from different endpoints, marking questionable files and actions as they occur.

- **Automated Incident Response**

  One of the main breakthroughs, which made it possible to respond to incidents much faster, is the adoption of AI in the detection, analysis, and even in the resolving of security threats. A security breach would usually go through a very lengthy and exhausting process of data gathering, incident analysis and remediation, where each step took a considerable time to finish. AI could significantly reduce the duration of this long and tedious process and at the same time, improve its accuracy by enabling quick and accurate responses.

  AI will instantly evaluate the risk in terms of size and severity, decide the appropriate response, and even suggest such measures as cutting off the impacted systems' communication or stopping the malicious action. This automation reduces the burden on the security crew massively by not only removing the monotonous tasks but also greatly lowering the chances of mistakes made by humans.

- **Enhanced Threat Intelligence**

  Manual collection and analysis of data, which took an enormous amount of time and was potentially error-prone, have been the principal sources of threat intelligence in the past. On the contrary, AI systems carry out continuous monitoring of various data sources such as network traffic, user behaviour, and external threat feeds, which results in the rapid and precise detection of potential threats. AI, in fact, helps in the revealing of new threats by spotting the odd activities and connecting them to the existing attack patterns.

  Moreover, the Artificial Intelligence systems are very much capable of collecting threat intelligence from various organizations and even security vendors, hence giving them a global overview of the threat landscape. This kind of consolidated intelligence allows the security staff to be always one step ahead of the intruders by getting to know the latest Tactics, Techniques, and Procedures (TTPs) of the criminals.

- **Remediation Guided by Generative AI**

  Generative AI employs the power of advanced machine learning models to carry out different types of attacks, evaluate their impact, and provide precise and effective countermeasures. Consequently, it enables organizations to set up customized remediation strategies which put into focus the nature of each threat.

  In addition, generative AI can assist in automating complex remediation jobs such as fixing software defects and adjusting security settings for the network. It is the AI systems that take over the human role in this process, hence, there is a major cut in the time taken to handle and resolve security incidents.

- **Security Questionnaire Automation**

  Automation driven by AI also makes it easier to complete security questionnaires, which are frequently requested during vendor assessments or compliance audits. The old way of doing it was that these questionnaires had to be filled in manually and it would take a lot of time because information had to be collected from different departments and the accuracy and currency of the responses had to be verified. In this scenario, AI could take over and do the extraction of relevant data from the internal documentation, and then provide responses that align with the organization's security policies and practices. AI also can support systems to always update the answers to security questionnaires as per new information; thus the responses will be accurate all the time.

1.5.2 Challenges of Implementing AI in Security

While improvement in security, AI-specific solutions also translate into more sophisticated challenges for their successful deployment:

- **False positives and the need for human intervention**: When Cybersecurity tools contact AI, they can create situations called false positives, which means that good actions are mistakenly identified as bad ones. Security experts had to scrutinize and ultimately remedy such problems, which might lead the team to experience exhaustion due to being in constant confrontation with the alerts.

- **Data privacy concerns**: The one main approach generally used by AI systems for this purpose has been behavior analytics for identifying anomalies and risk detection. However, the aforementioned technique still places data privacy issues as the most critical concern since it necessitates the user's actions to be observed and analyzed.
- **Resource and computational overhead**: Cybersecurity has embraced AI but it has done at the cost of tremendous power consumption and advanced tech. The processing of immense data and execution of intricate mathematical equations using AI methods call for a super-computer system along with equally powerful storage. Thus, the whole AI lifecycle from development to maintenance can be relatively high in terms of resources as it requires highly skilled personnel and financial backing for constant support.

1.5.3 Best Practices for Implementing AI in Cybersecurity

These are various ways through which companies can enhance the efficacy of cybersecurity by using AI.

1. Ensuring Data Quality and Privacy

The development of precise AI systems that are capable of identifying and responding to models of threats up to 2023 requires very good data. So, companies must give top priority to the data cleansing and validation processes in their daily operations to get rid of the errors and inconsistencies that would otherwise lead to poor AI performance.

In addition, the entities have to guarantee the confidentiality of their data. While the implementation of encryption, anonymization, and access control methods can help in protecting the sensitive data, they are also capable of preventing the threats. Furthermore, the compliance with the laws like GDPR and CCPA not only reduces the privacy issues but also increases the accountability and safety.

2. Integration with Existing Systems

The smooth addition of AI to the already existing security systems results in a significant increase in their overall efficiency and no interruptions in operations. It means making AI tools work together with the current infrastructures like firewalls, intrusion detection systems, and SIEM platforms.

By employing APIs and standard protocols, the smooth integration was achieved that allowed AI to work hand in hand with the traditional security measures. The complete testing at the time of integration confirms that AI is the one to help and not the one to obstruct the existing security operations.

3. Human-AI Collaboration

The whole concept of human-AI collaboration being effective came from the utilization of the strengths from both the sides, the AI and the human experts. AI is not only suitable for processing a great number of data but also for spotting patterns, however, the human control is very important to the understanding of the context and the making of the decision.

Using AI as an assistant instead of a replacement supports the aforementioned collaboration between human and machine. The security experts may then spend their time on tasks that require strategy while AI is doing the routine monitoring and analysis. The performance of AI can thus be made to improve continually owing to the regular training and feedback loops set up between AI systems and human operators.

4. Regularly Testing and Updating AI Models

Regularly testing and updating AI models are required to keep them efficient in a continually changing threat environment. Monitoring AI performance regularly allows the detection of areas needing improvement and also the prevention of model drift where AI gets less accurate with the passage of time.

Establishing a plan for retraining models using new data keeps them up-to-date with upcoming threats. Furthermore, adversarial testing can expose the weaknesses of AI models and consequently help organizations to strengthen them against possible invasions. Keeping AI models updated and sturdy is a prerequisite for having strong cybersecurity defenses.

Multiple Choice Questions (MCQs)

1. **What is the primary role of artificial intelligence (AI) in cybersecurity?**
    a. Replacing all Human Security Analysts
    b. Automating Hardware-Level Security Controls
    c. Enhancing Threat Detection and Response Through Intelligent Analysis
    d. Eliminating the Need for Security Policies
2. **Which of the following best defines machine learning in cybersecurity?**
    a. Programming Systems to Follow Fixed Security Rules
    b. Systems That Learn Patterns from Data to Detect Threats
    c. Encrypting Data Using Predefined Algorithms
    d. Monitoring Networks Manually for Suspicious Activity
3. **Which cyber threat uses deceptive emails to trick users into revealing sensitive information?**
    a. Malware
    b. Phishing
    c. DDoS
    d. SQL Injection

4. **Modern cyberattacks are more dangerous because they are:**
    a. Random and Unstructured
    b. Easily Detectable by Signature-Based Systems
    c. Automated, Adaptive, and Multi-Vector
    d. Limited to a Single Attack Surface
5. **In security analytics, what does the term features refer to?**
    a. Final Security Alerts
    b. Raw Unprocessed Data
    c. Measurable Attributes Extracted from Data for Analysis
    d. Visualization Dashboards
6. **Which type of data is most commonly used for training AI-Based intrusion detection systems?**
    a. Multimedia Data
    b. System and Network Log Data
    c. Social Media Data
    d. Financial Transaction Records
7. **What is a key limitation of traditional rule-based security systems?**
    a. High Computational Cost
    b. Inability to Handle Known Attacks
    c. Difficulty in Detecting Zero-Day or Unknown Attacks
    d. Excessive use of Encryption
8. **How do AI-driven security approaches improve over traditional methods?**
    a. By Relying Only on Predefined Attack Signatures
    b. By Adapting to New and Evolving Threat Patterns
    c. By Eliminating False Positives Entirely
    d. By Operating Without any Data

9. **One major challenge in applying AI to cybersecurity is:**
    a. Lack of Cybersecurity Threats
    b. Excess Availability of Labeled Data
    c. Data Imbalance and Poor-Quality Datasets
    d. Simplicity of Attack Patterns
10. **Which of the following is an ethical concern related to ai in cybersecurity?**
    a. Increased Processing Speed
    b. User Privacy and Data Protection
    c. High Storage Capacity
    d. Network Bandwidth Utilization

Answers

1	2	3	4	5	6	7	8	9	10
c	b	b	c	c	b	c	b	c	b

Chapter 2

Core AI Techniques and Architectures for Security

2.1 Machine Learning Models for Threat Detection

Machine learning is an AI technique that aims to help computers identify and classify data, find patterns within it, draw conclusions and make predictions, and uncover new insights. Systems continuously educate themselves to improve accuracy by sending historical data to algorithms that create machine learning models (Kaur et al., 2023).

The quality of a ML model is determined by two primary elements:

1. Accuracy of the data used (i.e., garbage in, garbage out)
2. The algorithm's suitability for the application

The following are a few examples of cybersecurity-related algorithmic machine learning applications:

- Decision tree algorithm—for the purpose of identifying and categorizing assaults
- Dimensionality reduction algorithms—the purpose of eliminating superfluous and unimportant information
- K-means clustering—used to identify malicious software
- K-nearest neighbors' classifier (KNN)—using face recognition technology for authentication purposes
- Linear regression— models for predicting how network security will work

- Logistic regression— to identify instances of fraud
- Naïve Bayes algorithm—in order to identify intrusions
- Random forest algorithm—in order to categorize phishing attempts
- Support Vector Machine (SVM) algorithm—in order to categorize, identify, and forecast IP and port numbers that are on blacklists

How machine learning transforms cybersecurity

The power of ML models to process and infer conclusions on the large volumes of data is what is driving the cybersecurity changes. The main limitation with traditional security tools is that they are mostly based on set of rules and known threat signatures and cannot identify new or emerging attacks.

Machine learning is transforming the approach to cybersecurity to offer adaptive and proactive protection. The threat landscape is ever-changing, and for this reason, the models developed to counter this threat are also changing such that organizations move towards predictive security postures as opposed to reactive security postures.

The goal of constantly feeding large datasets into machine learning models is to spot patterns and anomalies as they happen. Organisations can use these insights to spot emerging dangers, like zero-day attacks, before they do serious damage.

Machine learning is utilized for more than just detection; it also automates incident response and management. Cybersecurity systems powered by machine learning may identify risks in a flash and take targeted measures (like erasing infected systems from the network or blocking harmful IP addresses) when necessary. This lessens the potential harm and allows organisations to carry on in the event of an attack. This is helpful because security teams may reduce the amount of time spent investigating and containing problems by prioritizing notifications more efficiently.

2.1.1 Role of AI and machine learning in cybersecurity

The capacity to anticipate, identify, and react to dangers with unparalleled precision and velocity has led to AI and ML becoming essential parts of cybersecurity systems. AI and ML play critical roles in cybersecurity, including:

- Identifying trends and identifying irregularities that can be signs of security breach or attack.
- The automation of incident reactions and complicated security procedures
- Improvements to current cybersecurity safeguards
- Applying knowledge gained from both past and present data throughout time
- The detection of zero-day attacks and unknown malware
- The ability for defenses to react to new cyber threats based on past experiences
- Anticipating possible weak spots
- Improving safety measures by studying actual actions
- The use of fewer manual interventions
- Playing out potential assault scenarios

2.1.2 Machine learning in cybersecurity tools

1. **Anti-malware and anti-virus:** Apply ML approaches to analyze code, malware behaviour, or execution patterns in order to detect and identify malicious software, including zero-day threats.
2. **Cloud security posture management (CSPM):** Machine learning can also improve CSPM technologies by spotting suspect cloud activity, misconfigurations, and possible policy violations based on usage trends.

3. **Email security gateways:** AI can spot phishing, spoofing, and business email compromise by looking at the email's content, how the sender acts, and its URL structure.
4. **Endpoint detection and response (EDR):** Use machine learning to monitor endpoint traffic, identify risks based on attack signatures and odd behaviour, and more.
5. **Intrusion detection and prevention Systems (IDPS):** Apply ML to identify when data traversing the network is abnormal and block unauthorized access using information about attack signatures, even when unknown.
6. **Network traffic analysis:** Use machine learning to look for strange patterns in network flow data. This will help you find things like data leaks, command-and-control contact, and movement from one network to another.
7. **Security information and event management (SIEM):** ML can be used to analyze historical security event data for correlation, anomaly detection, and false positive reduction.
8. **Security orchestration, automation, and response (SOAR):** Prioritize alerts, propose or automate response actions based on behaviour and threat intelligence using ML.
9. **User and entity behavior analytics (UEBA):** Establish regular user and system behaviour baselines using machine learning, and then highlight suspicious activity that may suggest an attack from outside sources or hostile insiders.

2.1.3 Types of machine learning

1. Supervised machine learning in cybersecurity

Supervised ML has several uses in cybersecurity, including data classification and outcome prediction. It specifies the variables that will be used to test for correlations and uses labelled datasets to train algorithms using inputs and outputs provided. During cross-validation, the model changes its weights in response to input data in order to avoid overfitting and underfitting.

There are multiple applications of supervised ML in the field of cybersecurity, such as:

- Network threats, such scanning and spoofing, can be identified by their distinctive labels.
- The process of identifying potential security risks and making predictions or classifications based on a target variable.
- Model training using both benign and harmful samples to aid in the prediction of the maliciousness of fresh samples.

There are many more applications for supervised machine learning than just cybersecurity:

- Binary classification—sorting information into two groups
- Multi-class classification—picking a choice between more than two options
- Regression modeling—forecasting values that are continuous
- Ensemble learning—building a more precise forecast by integrating the outputs of various machine learning models

Examples of cybersecurity-related supervised ML techniques:

- Adaptive boosting
- Linear regression
- Logistic regression
- Naïve Bayes
- Neural networks
- Random forest
- Support Vector Machines (SVM)

2. Reinforcement machine learning in cybersecurity

Reinforcement learning, a subset of supervised learning, is utilized in cybersecurity. Reinforcement learning is an algorithm training method that uses trial and error rather than sample data. Training the algorithm to seek affirmation while avoiding punishment is the purpose of the technique, which entails recording and responding to positive or negative comments.

The field of cybersecurity makes use of reinforcement learning in various ways, such as:

- Machine learning (ML) model training for real-time attack detection and mitigation through adversarial simulation
- Autonomous intrusion detections
- Cyber-physical systems
- DDoS defenses

Machine learning has several applications outside of cybersecurity; one common one is reinforcement learning, which is utilized when:

- There is a known model of the environment, but there isn't an analytical solution.
- There is only an environmental simulation model provided.
- Engaging with the environment is the sole means of gathering its data.

Cybersecurity applications of reinforcement learning methods:

- Deep Deterministic
- Deep Q Network (DQN)
- Policy Gradient (DDPG)

3. Unsupervised machine learning in cybersecurity

Cybersecurity unsupervised ML uses picture and audio/video datasets, publications, and social media posts as examples of unlabeled data. Without any human intervention, it can detect hidden groups or patterns in data.

This approach is essentially a data set scan that seeks for patterns to use for subgroup classification. Unsupervised machine learning is a typical use case for DL.

There are a number of potential uses for unsupervised ML in cybersecurity, including:

- Detecting unusual behavior
- Identifying new attack patterns
- Mitigating zero-day attacks

ML has several applications beyond cybersecurity, one of which is unsupervised ML:

- Anomaly detection
- Association mining
- Clustering
- Dimensionality reduction (i.e., reducing the number of variables in a data set)

Cybersecurity applications of unsupervised machine learning:

- K-means clustering
- Neural networks
- Principal component analysis (PCA)
- Probabilistic clustering
- Singular value decomposition (SVD)

4. Semi-supervised machine learning in cybersecurity

Hybrid ML for cybersecurity uses both supervised and uncontrolled methods. In situations where supervised learning algorithms do not have sufficient labelled data, it extracts a smaller collection of labelled data from a bigger quantity of unlabeled data for classification and feature extraction. Data sets are also labelled using it when the expense of doing so is prohibitive.

Cybersecurity applications of semi-supervised machine learning include:

- Adversarial neural networks
- Malicious and benign bot identification

- Malware detection
- Ransomware detection

The field of cybersecurity is just one of many where semi-supervised learning has found use beyond ML:

- Fraud detection
- Labeling data
- Machine translation

Some semi-supervised learning techniques used in cybersecurity:

- Consistency regularization
- Label propagation
- Pseudo-labeling
- Self-training

2.1.4 Benefits of machine learning in cybersecurity

- Facilitates the safe implementation of BYOD and CYOD policies.
- Automates cybersecurity processes
- Detects threats earlier and improves their detecting capabilities
- Makes proactive and adaptive defense systems possible
- Reduces response and danger detection times
- Determines obscure security holes in a network
- Prevents assaults with same features by incorporating lessons learnt from past attacks
- Streamlines the process of attack detection, prioritization, and remediation for security analysts
- Minimizes human errors
- Managing intricate identification systems that employ technologies such as voice recognition, motion detection, fingerprint scanning, retinal scanners, and facial recognition.

- Supports the avoidance of endpoint security risks
- Offers valuable insights into sophisticated dangers
- Reduces workloads
- Identifies malware by scanning large volumes of data
- Uses subtleties of typical behaviour to pick up on the tiniest deviations.

2.2 Deep Learning Architectures in Security

A branch of AI, DL is a subset of ML, the larger area of ML. The foundation of deep learning is an artificial neural network (ANN) programmed to mimic the structure and functions of the human brain. levels are necessary for these networks to take in and process data of varying complexity, which is why "deep" in this context indicates numerous levels. An example of an ANN is the CNN, which is most often used for computer vision applications.

The standard design for DL architectures often entails passing input data through multiple layers, with each layer performing a modification, and finally producing an output, such a prediction. Deep learning model development and exploration tools like TensorFlow and PyTorch provide a wealth of resources for beginners. On the other hand, a lot of processing power is needed for training. Since its foundation in graphics processing units (GPUs), which have recently grown more affordable and efficient, deep learning has found widespread use, particularly in cybersecurity.

2.2.1 Common Cybersecurity Threats

Cybersecurity experts often face the following threats:

- **Malware**: A wide variety of malicious applications designed to compromise various systems, networks, and devices fall under this general definition.
- **Data Breaches**: These happen when unauthorised people get a hold of confidential information, such company or personal records, and endanger everyone involved.

- **Social Engineering**: Cybercriminals frequently employ psychological manipulation as a means to get sensitive information or login credentials from individuals who are unaware of the danger. Along with other types of cyberattacks, these tactics could be used.
- **Phishing**: Phishing is a prevalent kind of social engineering that uses deceptive email messages that seem to have come from trusted sources to fool victims into giving over sensitive information or installing harmful programs.
- **SQL Injection**: Because it enables a hacker to do things like coerce the server into disclosing information or conducting malicious actions, this approach is focused on SQL servers.
- **Denial-of-Service** (**DoS**) **Attacks**: In these types of attacks, the perpetrator overwhelms a system with traffic to the point that it becomes unavailable to legitimate users.
- **Insider Threats**: Individuals with inside knowledge of a company, such as employees or even contractors, pose a hazard since they could be involved in the intentional or unintentional disclosure of sensitive information.
- **Advanced Persistent Threats (APTs)**: These attacks are new and sophisticated; they are undetectable and can bypass traditional security measures to infiltrate a network and collect intelligence before launching an assault.

2.2.2 Challenges in Traditional Cybersecurity

A larger attack surface and more complex and new threats have altered the cybersecurity landscape. The security solutions that were used in the past like firewalls and antivirus software rely largely on known threats and usually depict the signature-based detection system. Nevertheless, the approaches are also limited:

- **Static Detection:** It is true that there are disadvantages inherent in some of the traditional methods, particularly when it comes to the definition of new or unknown threat that can pose a threat to the networks.
- **High False Alarms:** The majority of security solutions used throughout history generate numerous false alarms which security experts depend on to conceal the actual threats.
- **Manual Intervention:** Traditional methods rely heavily on human intervention, rendering them slow in responding to an increasing threat.

Important uses of Deep Learning in IT Security

DL is applicable in many areas of cybersecurity, which includes but are not limited to:

- **Intrusion Detection Systems (IDS):** The DL models are able to check the traffic and identify attempted intrusions to make a clear distinction between normal and possible attacks.
- **Malware Detection:** DL algorithms on file behaviour analysis and its features can also be used to detect malware and different types of malwares.
- **Phishing Detection:** DL can be used to supplement the traditional methods of filtering email, analyzing the text in the message and identifying phishing attacks through slight patterns.
- **Behavioral Analytics:** Deep learning insight has one of the best functionalities of detecting abnormal activities of end-users that are deep rooted and regarded as insiders or whose accounts have been compromised.

Traditional vs. Modern Cybersecurity Framework

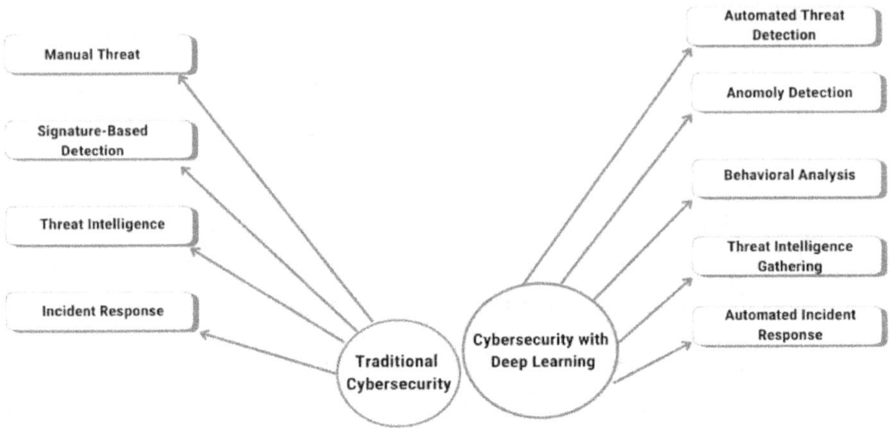

Figure 2.1: Traditional vs. Modern Cybersecurity Framework

Source: (Gill, 2024)

Deep Learning Architecture in Cybersecurity

A proper infrastructure that supports data collecting, learning models, and threat detection is essential for integrating deep learning into cybersecurity. Here, it shows a simplified flow diagram of a potential cybersecurity system that uses deep learning:

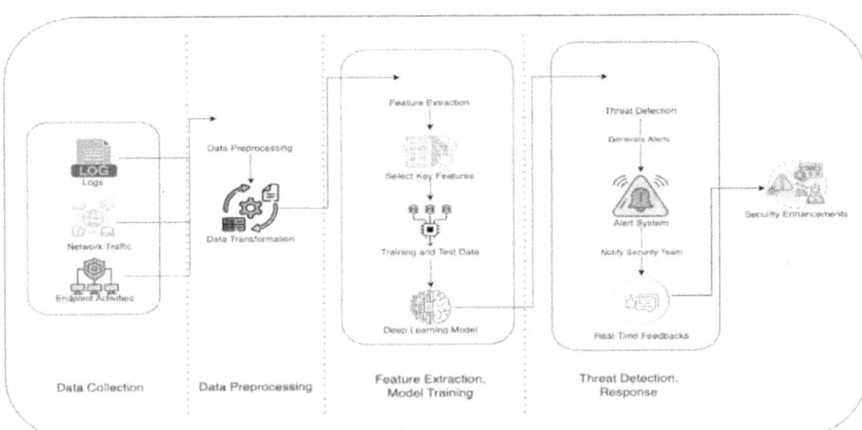

Figure 2.2: Deep Learning Architecture for Cybersecurity

Source: (Gill, 2024)

- **Data Collection**: Security data can be acquired from a variety of sources, including network traffic, computers, devices, and logos.
- **Data Preprocessing**: Machine learning models can be used to the modified and organized raw data that has been collected.
- **Model Training**: This study trains deep learning models to identify cyber threats using tagged datasets.
- **Threat Detection**: Additionally, trained programs analyze data flow and identify suspicious activities for further investigation.

Applications of Deep Learning in Cybersecurity

The field of AI is transforming nearly every industry. The AI technique known as DL is driving innovation in the IT sector and has limitless potential uses, from improving cancer detection and diagnosis to enhancing object recognition in autonomous car systems. Next, we'll examine a few of the cyber security applications of deep learning that were previously highlighted:

1. Intrusion Detection and Prevention Systems (IDS/IPS)

These systems are able to identify suspicious network activity, block unauthorised users, and notify the user when an intrusion has occurred. In most cases, generic attack forms and known signatures can identify them. In the face of dangers such as data breaches, this is helpful.

In the past, ML techniques were used to accomplish this. Unfortunately, security staff had to put in a lot of extra effort and suffered needless weariness because the system produced so many false-positives due to these algorithms.

Security teams may improve traffic analysis accuracy, decrease false alarm frequency, and differentiate between helpful and harmful network activity with the use of DL, CNNs, and RNNs. The end consequence might be ID/IP systems that are smarter.

Noteworthy solutions include WAF, Next-Generation Firewall (NGFW), and UEBA.

2. Dealing with Malware

The signature-based detection system is the backbone of traditional malware solutions, such ordinary firewalls. The business keeps track of potential threats and adds new ones to an existing database. Despite its effectiveness against simple dangers, this method is not up to the task of dealing with more sophisticated ones.

Instead of depending on memorizing existing fingerprints and typical attack patterns, deep learning systems may identify more complex threats. On the contrary, they become proficient with the system and are able to spot unusual behaviour that could be a sign of malicious actors or malware.

3. Spam and Social Engineering Detection

NLP, a type of DL, can make it easy to find spam and other types of social engineering and stop them. In order to identify and prevent spam, NLP learns typical patterns of speech and language and employs a number of statistical models.

4. Network Traffic Analysis

The use of DL ANNs to inspect HTTPS network traffic for signs of malicious activity has shown encouraging results. This is incredibly useful in the fight against various cyber threats, such as SQL injections and denial of service assaults.

5. User Behavior Analytics

A crucial security practice for every organization is monitoring and analyzing user actions and behaviour. Due to the fact that it evades security measures and frequently does not generate any warnings or alarms, it is far more difficult to detect than conventional harmful actions targeting the networks.

For instance, many cyber defense solutions are ineffective against insider threats, which happen when employees utilize their lawful access maliciously rather than invading the system from the outside.

One effective defense against these kinds of assaults is UEBA, or User and Entity Behaviour Analytics. It takes some time for it to learn typical staff habits, but after that, it can see suspicious activity, like logging into the system at odd hours, that could be an indication of an insider attack and trigger alarms.

2.3 Reinforcement Learning for Adaptive Defense

Adaptive defense RL is merely the question of how to teach a system to learn rather than adhere to set rules throughout its lifetime. The system monitors the types of attacks or threats that occur and attempts various defense measures, and then examines what succeeded and what failed. When response will minimize the damage or end an attack, it will be rewarded and have a higher probability of repeating the same action in future. In case of failure, the system is trained not to use that method. This will eventually enable the defense mechanism to adapt itself to the changing threats rather than remain stagnant by relying on the old protection systems. Simply put, it is a security system that learns and makes mistakes and gradually becomes smarter in protecting itself.

Reinforcement learning is easily applied to other cybersecurity contexts due to this learning methodology. One can add new reinforcement models, like intrusion detection, spam filtering, or malware response, to provide the system with the ability to respond to a variety of attacks concurrently. These models can be enhanced or integrated without having to redesign the whole defense configuration as cyber threats continue to evolve. This brings reinforcement learning as a flexible option, as I can append on reinforcement models in cyber systems to enhance security and maintain defenses adaptive to novel and changing attacks.

2.3.1 Reinforcement model in cyber

a. Deep Q-Networks

DQN is a concept that enables computers to learn from experience, much as how one can improve their gaming skills via repeated practice. It has a "memory" for its successful prior actions and a "brain" (a neural network) for its best-case scenario prediction. No matter if it's winning a game or preventing a cyberattack, it finds the optimal way to do it by trying different things and learning from its successes and failures. From Q-Learning, Q-Network was born. Gaining a policy that directs the agent's behaviour in certain situations to maximize rewards is the main objective of Q-learning. In Figure 2.3, Q-Network is an example of Q-learning that makes use of neural networks.

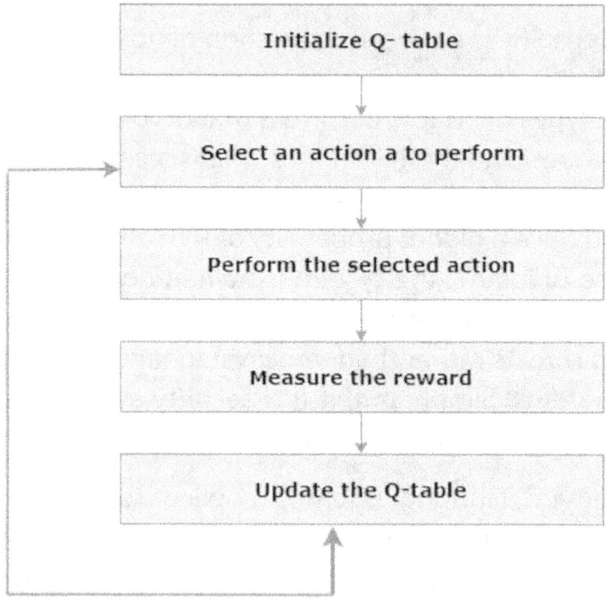

Figure 2.3: Visual representation of Q-learning

Source: (Loza, 2025)

Automated threat hunting involves sifting through mountains of network logs and event data in search of suspicious activity; intrusion detection systems (IDS) use it to decide whether to permit or deny a connection based on observed behaviour; and cyberattack simulation and defense optimization use it to learn how to react to different attack scenarios in order to reduce vulnerabilities.

b .Proximal Policy Optimization

A machine learning model called Proximal Policy Optimization (PPO) can learn to make smart judgements by experimenting and improving with rewards. It is also able to correct its strategy therefore it does not go wrong when learning which makes it remain steady and efficient. PPO is mainly applied to robots or games to teach the robots to behave in complicated circumstances, such as walking or playing chess in Figure 2.4.

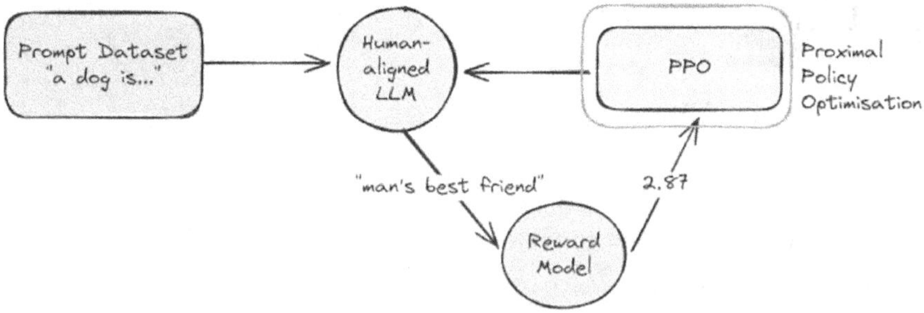

Figure 2.4: Visual representation of PRO

Source: (Loza, 2025)

Cybersecurity PPO can train systems to defend against attacks by simulating different kinds of attacks and figuring out what countermeasures work best, such preventing malicious traffic or identifying and removing affected devices.

C. Soft Actor-Critic

SAC is a ML model that tries to decide the choice by balancing the two tasks: receiving the best rewards and exploration of choices. It attempts to ensure that it does not merely adhere to the precautionary steps but also experiment to get even more significant solutions (Figure 2.5). Its adaptability and efficiency make it ideal for controlling autonomous vehicles, robots, or spotting suspicious patterns in cybersecurity.

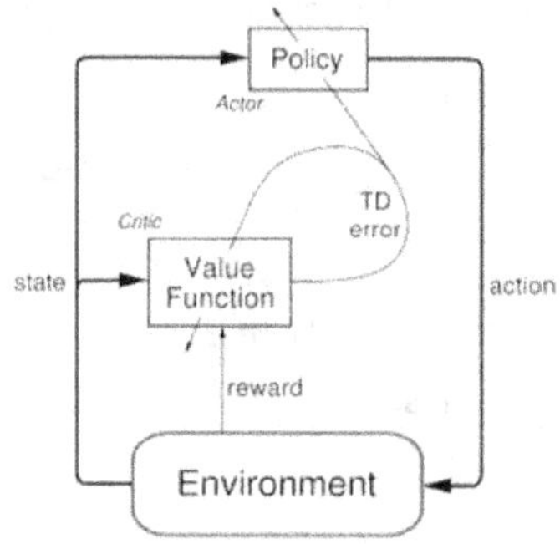

Figure 2.5: Visual representation of Actor-Critic architecture

Source: (Loza, 2025)

The algorithm finds its applications in IDSs, automated incident response, and endpoint protection. As an illustration, in the case of a ransomware attack, SAC might choose to shut down the affected systems, but impose minimum damage on other processes.

2.3.2 Pros and Cons of Reinforcement Learning

Advantages

- Adaptive learning Adaptive learning is a model that continually learns and evolves with changing conditions, and is therefore suitable in dynamic cybersecurity situations such as the development of new attack techniques or zero-day threats.
- Autonomous decision-making, in which agents have the capability of automating their responses to threats, eliminating the necessity of the human oversight, such as seizing automatically compromised devices in a network.
- Innovation of new solutions. That promotes exploration, enabling new vectors of attack or defensive strategy to be found which traditional models would have overlooked.
- Reduces overall network risk is an example of a goal that calls for long-term planning since it maximizes long-term strategies by focusing on cumulative benefits.
- Network security is one example of a high-dimensional, continuous environment that can benefit from this, since the states and activities in this setting are constantly changing.
- Real-time response. Agents are also able to identify and react to threats in real time and provide quicker mitigation compared to conventional methods.
- Multi-agent collaboration In this case, the model can collaborate with multiple agents (e.g. firewalls, IDS) to collaboratively enhance the overall security posture.
- Security teams can tailor RL models to their organization's needs, such as prioritizing the protection of critical assets,

using customizable incentive systems that grant them access to certain reward functions.

Disadvantages

- Compelling computer requirements. Especially in big and/ or complicated contexts, training models can be time-and computational-intensive.
- Data scarcity for training. These demands simulated or real environments to train but developing realistic cybersecurity simulation may be difficult and costly.
- Instability in training. The complexity of the environment or an ill-defined reward function might cause model instability.
- Exploration vs. Exploitation trade-off. Reinforcement models have the potential to make dangerous or suboptimal judgements when exploring, which could compromise the process or cause disruptions.
- Inability to interpret where models tend to be black boxes and security teams may not be able to comprehend how it arrived at a particular decision.
- Extrapolation of models trained in simulations to real-life conditions can lead to over-fitting to the simulated environment, as conditions vary in real life.
- Risk of misaligned rewards. This invalidates poorly constructed reward mechanisms and may result in undesirable behavior, including the attention to minor activities rather than mitigating against critical threats.
- Limited use in static problems. Reinforcement learning also doesn't work well for simple tasks like identifying malware; supervised learning models work better for these kinds of tasks.

2.3.3 Reinforcement Learning Applications in Threat Mitigation

The introduction of AI and RL in particular has transformed the environment of cybersecurity radically. The rule-based security is not always capable of providing the required protection with the ever-changing and sophisticated threats. Reinforcement learning, which has been able to learn and adapt to experience has been one of the potent weapons in the arsenal of the threat mitigation strategy. The dynamism model allows the security systems to improve and regenerate continuously with what has been found to be working or failed in responding to the security threats, and generate a more advanced security mechanism of responding to the threats. Application of RL in security systems is a reactive to proactive shift in reducing threats, and the capacity of systems to predict and prevent any potential security breach before it takes place. The complexity of the modern cyber threats, along with the rate of their evolution, demand clever systems with the ability to make autonomous decisions and act promptly - which the RL systems can quite efficiently provide. The combination of the reinforcement learning and the security has opened new possibilities in curbing threats and to date, organizations have managed to develop more flexible and adaptive security infrastructures.

- **Intrusion Detection and Prevention in Network**

  Reinforcement learning has been used in network security and this has changed the manner in which organizations identify and prevent intrusion. Even though the classical signature-based detection algorithms can possibly be efficient in coping with the known threats, they are usually prone to pseudo-zero-day attacks and face the unknown threat vectors. This weakness is countered by using RL-based systems that will monitor network traffic and keep their mechanisms constantly updated in line with the network traffic trend. These are systems which have advanced algorithm that analyses the data on the packets, characteristics of the network flows and user behavior patterns in order to identify potential threats.

- **Malware Detection and Classification**

  Reinforcement learning has also been found to be highly efficient in detecting and classifying malwares. The modern malware is dynamic; it is able to evolve and modify itself and this aspect is a huge obstacle to the traditional methods of noticing the malware. The malware detectors (using the RL) utilize their learning capabilities to acquire the behavioral profiles and characteristics of different types of malwares. These systems probe and address a wide variety of features, including the code formatting, API calls, system modification and network communication patterns, in order to create an overall profile of threats.

- **Automated Incident Response**

  Introduction of reinforcement learning in incident response systems has transformed how security breach and threats are addressed in organizations. What is learnt with these automated systems is the effective response strategies through interacting with various types of security incidents, thereby, makes it intelligent in decision making. The RL agents take into account different resolutions and the potential outcomes and select the most efficient course of action based on the examination of a specific case and the severity of the event. The reduction of response time and delivery of appropriate and consistent measures on different types of security incidents is highly influenced by this automated solution.

- **Authentication and Access Control**

  The use of reinforcement learning in threat hunting has enabled a shift of organizations to proactive security postures instead of reacting to security. The RLs-based threat hunting systems receive vast amounts of security data to identify the potential threat prior to it being converted into a real attack. These systems are able to detect low-level compromising indicators and trends that can be a pointer to looming security threats. The RL agents also build up advanced hunting policy by prioritizing territories of exploration based on a potential danger and prior history of attack. This kind of strategy will enable the management of security resources in a more efficient way since this method can attract attention to the most likely sources of possible threats.

- **Pre-Crime and Threat Hunting**

  Reinforcement learning in threat hunting has allowed organizations to transform their security postures to proactive ones. Threat hunting systems that function under the RL paradigm constantly process large volumes of security data to determine the possible existence of threats before they transform into real attacks. Those systems are taught to identify the very slippery signs of compromise and patterns that may indicate the threat of security issues. The RL agents build advanced hunting techniques and areas of inquiry are given precedence depending on the possible risk level and previous attack patterns. Such a way would allow to devote more attention to security resource allocation, as it would be possible to concentrate on the most probable sources of potential threats.

- **DDoS Attack Mitigation**

  Reinforcement learning philosophy has changed the state of art of DDoS attacks mitigation by developing more complex and dynamic defense processes. By continuously observing the network activity and other characteristics of the traffic the RL-based systems are trained to distinguish between legitimate traffic and attacks. These systems develop dynamic mitigation systems that can adapt with the changing pattern of attacks as well as new versions of DDoS attacks. The RL agents are conditioned to achieve a balance between the need to adequately counter attack and the need to make the services available to the legitimate users and maximize their response actions. The high-tech mitigation systems can coordinate response on both multifaceted layers of the network and geographical span providing complete security against distributed attacks.

- **Endpoint Protection**

  Reinforcement learning has significantly benefited the security of individual devices as well as network endpoints as far as endpoint protection is concerned. The endpoint protection systems that are learned with the help of RL are trained to identify and respond to the threats by constantly monitoring the behavior of the devices and the trends of activities. These systems develop wholesome protection mechanisms that encompass the different aspects of endpoint protection including process protection, file system protection and the network communication.

- **Social Engineering Defense**

  The development of more effective detection and prevention systems for social engineering attacks has been greatly enhanced by reinforcement learning. The RL-based systems are trained to identify potential social engineering attacks based on communication characteristics and contents and user behavior. These systems generate sophisticated detection measures that have the ability to identify advanced phishing and other social engineering techniques. The RL agents will be trained to detect the light indicators of ill intent with most minimum false positives that will impact truthful communications. The defense mechanisms, which are highly developed, can adjust their detection strategies to the newly appeared type of attack, as well as to the new types of social engineering.

2.4 Anomaly Detection and Unsupervised Learning Techniques

A phenomenon is just something that is unusual, does not conform to the established pattern or is unusual by being different in a particular category or situation. In order to be able to explain it easily, we shall take some bright examples:

There are a lot of iPhones out there, mostly Samsung ones, and then there is the iPhone. One exception is the iPhone, which serves as a brand differentiator.

Assume that among the several pens you are given, one is a fountain pen as opposed to a standard ball point pen. Because it differs from the norm, the fountain pen is an outlier.

What is anomaly detection?

Anomaly identification is a technique for locating data points that deviate significantly from the norm or are considered outliers in a dataset.

Anomaly detection involves the detection of an anomaly, which is not perceived as normal or expected in historical or known data, and it is based on the previous information about what happens to be normal. It is critical towards the quality and safety of the data in a wide range of domains.

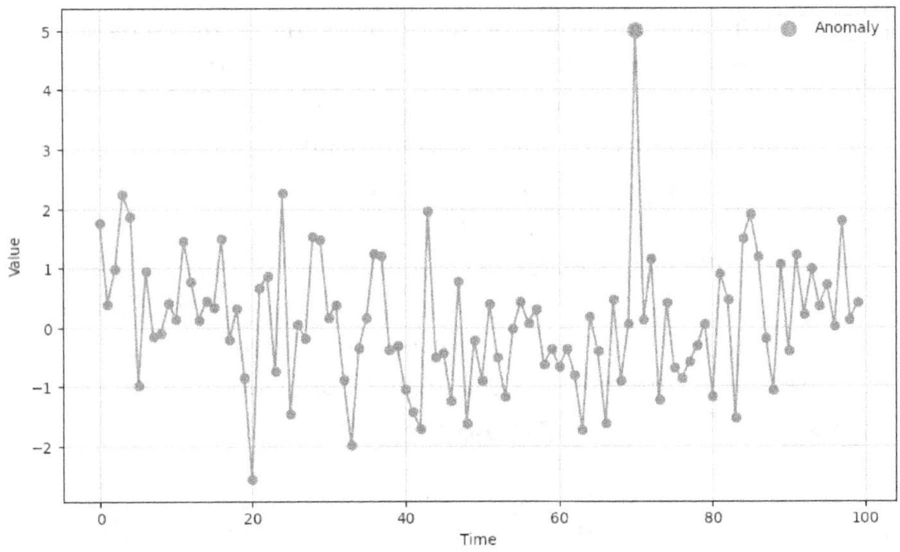

Figure 2.6: Anomaly Detection Example

Source: (Hiraltalsaniya, 2023)

2.4.1 Anomaly Detection use Cases

Here are a few varied uses for machine learning anomaly detection:

- Event detection in sensor networks
- Manufacturing quality control
- Healthcare monitoring
- Social media monitoring

- Fraud detection
- Network intrusion detection
- Healthcare monitoring
- Insurance claim analysis
- Cybersecurity threat detection
- Identity theft
- Traffic monitoring
- Network intrusion detection
- Data breaches
- Intrusion detection
- Video surveillance

2.4.2 Three settings for anomaly detection

1. Supervised Anomaly Detection:

Train the anomaly detection model with this setup's labelled dataset, where every data item is unambiguously tagged as normal or anomalous. By learning from the outcomes of typical data, the model can spot outliers in novel, unknown data. In cases when abnormalities are easily characterized and detected, and where you have a high-quality labelled dataset to train on, supervised anomaly detection might be useful.

ML Algorithm for structured data:

- Bayesian networks
- k-nearest neighbors (KNN)
- Decision trees

2. Clean Anomaly Detection:

A situation where clean anomaly detecting is applicable is when the data is generally free of noise and mistakes, making the anomaly detection process easier. Identifying out-of-the-ordinary deviations from the established norms is the primary focus here. Whenever the data is organised and shows predictable patterns, like when trying to detect fraud in a financial transaction or regulate quality in a manufacturing process, clean anomaly detection is usually used.

3. Unsupervised Anomaly Detection:

Unsupervised anomaly detection is where no labeled anomalies are present in the training data and the model must determine the presence of anomalies without prior information as to what is an anomaly. The task of the model is to locate data points which are far apart as compared to most of the data and thus it is applicable in situations where anomalies are infrequent or poorly known.

ML algorithm for unstructured data:

- K-means
- One-class support vector machine

2.4.3 Common approaches to anomaly detection

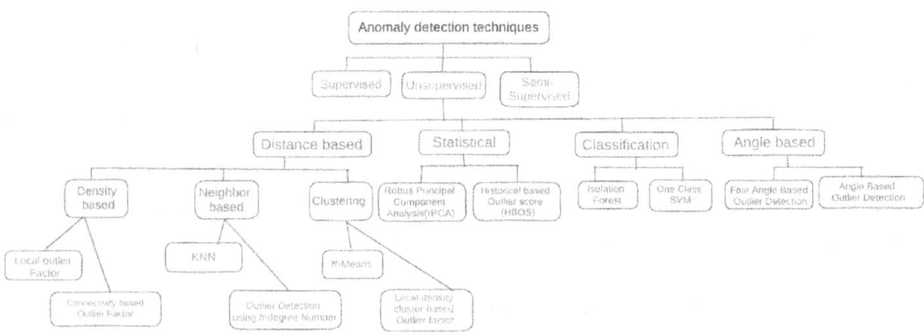

Figure 2.7: Anomaly Detection Techniques

Source: (Agarwal, 2024)

1. Statistical methods:

- **Z-Score/Standard Score**: This technique calculates the dispersion of a data set around its mean, often known as the standard deviation. Any data point that deviates greatly from the average is considered an outlier.

- **Percentiles**: Anomaly identification using percentiles or quantiles, where values below or above a threshold are deemed outliers.

2. Machine learning algorithms:

- **Isolation Forest**: A tree-based ensemble learning technique that isolates anomalies in the most effective way.
- **One-Class SVM**: The ability to train a support vector machine classifier to differentiate between typical and exceptional data.
- **K-Nearest Neighbors (KNN)**: The distance from the point to its KNNs determines the anomaly score; points that are farther away are deemed more suspicious.
- **Autoencoders**: Using reconstruction error to detect outliers, neural networks trained to learn a reduced data representation.

3. Clustering methods:

- **DBSCAN (Density-Based Spatial Clustering of Applications with Noise)**: Sorts data points into groups based on their density; anything that doesn't fit into any of the groups is considered an outlier.
- **K-Means Clustering**: Anomalies are data points that don't fit well into any predetermined categories.

4. Time-series analysis:

- **Moving Averages**: Anomaly detection using standard deviations from moving averages and exponential moving averages.
- **Seasonal Decomposition**: Anomalies are typically found in the residual component after the process of splitting a time series into its trend and seasonal components.

5. Proximity-based approaches:

- **Mahala Nobis Distance**: This function examines the relationships between attributes to determine the distance between data points and the distribution center.

- **Local Outlier Factor (LOF)**: Identifies regions with diverse densities by calculating the relative local density deviation of data points.

2.5 Hybrid, Ensemble, and Multi-Modal AI Systems

It is important to understand the differences and complements between hybrid, ensemble and multi-modal AI systems to have appreciation of the subtle scenery of the current artificial intelligence. Although they all seek to expand the abilities of AI beyond the limits of a single-model, they do so with a completely different understanding of the problem. A hybrid system attempts to combine different AI methods or models in a complementary way to solve a complicated problem, and use the merits of each component; an ensemble approach aims to combine predictions of multiple similar or different models trained to do the same task in order to achieve higher accuracy and stability; and a multi-modal system is specially designed to process, understand, and correlate information between different types of data, such as text, images, and sound, within a single system. This facilitates a more sound and context-centered way of dealing with the complex and real-world situations.

The main concern of hybrid and ensemble systems is the structural integration of various computational methods or models in order to tackle a given task in a more efficient way that no single method would allow individually. A hybrid AI is usually a combination of a different methodology, such as a rule-based system of reasoning which is symbolic and a statistical machine learning model to achieve a trade-off between interpretability and flexibility.

The logic constraint aspect may be dealt with by the rule-based aspect whereas the machine learning component may detect the intricate data patterns. Ensemble learning in contrast uses multiple individual models to do the same task to be predicted with the result being averaged, voted upon, stacked, etc. to minimize variance and bias in the eventual prediction. It is a late fusion wherein there is marshaling of decisions at the output level, although a hybrid model can involve more extensive interaction at any of the levels of the architecture.

2.5.1 Hybrid AI System

Hybrid AI is an advanced technology solution which incorporates the use of various AI technology types to peak their capabilities, functionality, flexibility and problem-solving.

The goal of developing AI in a hybrid fashion is to build systems that are better at reasoning, learning, and adaptability than AI systems that have not been merged. These systems can include rule-based symbolic reasoning, machine learning, and deep learning, among others.

This approach not only improves the efficiency of operations and gives better insights to business owners in many domains, but it also allows AI systems to integrate the advantages of several methodologies, making solutions easier to interpret and scale.

Types of hybrid AI

Now that we've talked about what hybrid AI is, let's talk about the different kinds of hybrid AI and what they can do.

The most common type of artificial intelligence (AI) nowadays is hybrid AI, which incorporates aspects of many AI tactics. These strategies can include symbolic AI and machine learning, neural networks and knowledge graphs, or deep learning and reinforcement learning.

Each combination possesses its merit, either it is the formation of reasoning ability, choice or adjustment to complex situations.

- **Symbolic AI and machine learning**

  Rule-based AI, sometimes called symbolic AI, is concerned with solving problems with the help of logic and explicit rules. It is good at reasoning, processing and interpreting structured data but poor at unstructured data processing and processing of large-scale problems.

Machine learning (ML) is data-oriented, however, and it is good at recognizing and predicting patterns. It is efficient in combination with big data, finding tendencies without having any specific guidelines. Notwithstanding, ML models can be hard to interpret, and they might not be effective at solving problems that demand logical arguments.

Hybrid AI, which combines ML with symbolic AI, takes advantage of ML's predictive power and symbolic systems' reasoning power. An example would be a system that would apply symbolic AI to adhere to medical principles in the diagnosis of a patient, whereas machine learning would analyze records of patients and test findings and give them personalized advice.

- **Neural networks and knowledge graphs**

Deep learning models, particularly neural networks, are highly effective in finding patterns in massive datasets that contain images, text, and audio. Having said that, they aren't usually able to reason or understand how everything is connected.

Knowledge graphs represent the information in a manner that gives information on the relationship between different concepts, with better context and reasoning. They also explain the relationships between entities, and this makes them applicable in applications that need contextual awareness.

Neural networks are capable of operating on big volumes of unstructured data when hybrid AI is applied and knowledge graphs are used in understanding the connection among various pieces of data. The combination strengthens the ability to make decisions and enables one to have a more detailed appreciation of hard to interpret information.

A customer support system is one example, where neural networks could analyze the interaction between the customer and the system, and a knowledge graph can give the system an understanding of what the customer likes and what has gone wrong previously to offer an improved solution.

- **Deep learning and reinforcement learning**

  DL systems are great at deriving patterns out of massive datasets but generally have a high training data requirement to work well. Conversely, RL, is a type of learning that entails the interaction with an environmental system via reinforcement and punishment that is accorded based on actions. Nevertheless, this kind of programmed may fail in case of excessive complexity without instructions.

  In a hybrid approach, DL may be applied to look into the environment and identify any patterns that are of interest, whereas the reinforcement learning of the system allows it to learn the best methods by trial and error.

  An illustration is that deep learning could be used to make a robot recognize objects, and reinforcement learning could be used to teach the robot how to manipulate that object in a manner that optimizes its performance on a task.

2.5.2 Components of Hybrid AI

Hybrid AI, as the term implies, is a methodology that incorporates various AI approaches and methods. This is aimed at developing a stronger and more efficient AI system to address a broader scope of tasks more effectively. A hybrid AI system can be constructed with varying main components based on the objectives of the system, yet can include some or all of the following:

1. **Symbolic AI (Declarative AI):** This subfield of artificial intelligence focusses on developing models and systems with the ability to think rationally and adhere to predetermined rules. System inferences are governed by a set of rules typically developed by human experts. The members of this subset comprise:

   - **Expert systems:** These are machines programmed to mimic human intelligence. Instead of the typical computer code, they tackle complex issues by using a great deal of information, primarily through the use of if-then logic. Expert humans have pre-programmed the "knowledge".

- **Business Rules Management Systems (BRMS):** Automating and managing business rules is made easier with BRMS. To make decisions based on changeable rules without modifying the system code, these solutions allow enterprises to use them.

2. **Machine learning (Non-declarative AI):** A subset of data called "training data" is used by machine learning algorithms to build a mathematical framework. Afterwards, this framework is used to generate predictions or judgements, all without requiring direct coding to carry out the particular operation. This branch includes:

   - **Decision tree learning:** Classification and regression are two applications of decision trees as models. A leaf node in a tree-like structure represents an option, an interior node represents an attribute, and a branch shows the test's conclusion.

   - **Deep learning:** A branch of machine learning known as deep learning architectures uses ANNs and other multi-layer ANNs to make predictions. A number of cutting-edge domains have benefited greatly from these methods, including object detection, visual object identification, and speech recognition.

   - **Neural networks:** The complex network architecture of animal brains serves as an inspiration for the creation of these computer systems. One class of ML models that aims to mimic how the brain works is pattern recognition algorithms.

   - **Bayesian networks:** Belief networks and Bayesian networks are two names for the same kind of probabilistic graphical model that uses DAGs to depict variables and the conditions under which they are dependent. When trying to determine the possible causes of an event based on known information, Bayesian networks excel.

   - **Support vector machines:** Classification, regression, and outlier identification are just a few of the many applications of Support Vector Machines (SVMs), a type of supervised learning technology. Because a variety of Kernel functions can be selected for decision-making, SVMs provide adaptability and perform well in environments with numerous dimensions.

However, hybrid AI uses a mix of these approaches to make a more complete and effective AI system. It minimizes the shortcomings of various systems while capitalizing on the strengths of each technique. A hybrid AI system has the ability to learn new things, adapt to new situations, and solve complex problems. It can also perform a wider range of tasks.

2.5.3 Types of AI that form the Hybrid AI ecosystem

The Hybrid Intelligence ecosystem includes the following forms of AI:

- **Adaptive AI:** Adaptive AI is a type of AI that changes its behaviour and reactions in response to new information and observations. The capacity to alter one's actions in response to fresh data is what sets adaptive AI apart from conventional computer systems that blindly follow established protocols. This form of AI is not programmed with all the solutions; it is actually learning as it goes through its experiences and adjusts its operations and decision-making patterns to reach its goals, effectively learning in the process.
- **Learning AI:** Learning AI is a field of artificial intelligence that can flourish on data to enhance its productivity. The peculiarity of the AI based learning is that it does not need to be explicitly programmed to increase its capabilities and performance. Instead, it uses the data it has been fed on or collected to self-improve refining its predictions or outputs through time.
- **General AI:** The term "general AI" refers to a certain type of AI that can mimic human intelligence and do every mental operation a person could. It is a speculative idea currently, referring to a system that has the potential to recreate the intelligence capabilities of humans, including but not confined to natural language processing, representation of knowledge, problem-solving and planning.

- **Narrow AI:** A type of artificial intelligence known as weak AI or narrow AI is one that is trained to do just one or a small number of tasks successfully. Included in this category might be AI systems that can play chess, operate cars, or provide online product recommendations. Systems like these are designed to excel in specific domains, but they lack the adaptability that people possess.
- **Parallel AI:** The term "parallel AI" describes AI systems that make use of the processing power of numerous computers running in parallel. By distributing the processing load over a cluster of computers, these AI systems can efficiently handle massive datasets and complex algorithms.
- **Specialized AI:** Specialized AI is tailored to deliver explicit attention to a problem or task. These may include the medical condition diagnosis through symptoms and medical visuals, predicting stock market patterns and even interpolating natural languages. Specialized AI is effective in its area, but it might not be very effective in other areas.
- **Symbiotic AI:** Symbiotic AI is an idea in which various AI systems will cooperate and exchange knowledge with one another. Combining these AI systems will enable them to accomplish more complicated tasks or comprehend larger contexts than any single one of them.
- **Virtual AI:** The only places where virtual AI can exist are on digital devices, like computers or cellphones. Game AI, chatbots, and virtual assistants such as Alexa and Siri are all forms of virtual AI. These artificial intelligence systems engage in user interactions, data processing, and task execution within their virtual environments.

2.5.4 Importance of Ensemble AI System

The relevance of an ensemble AI system is that it takes a set of models rather than a single model based on the idea that it will somehow figure it out. The models have their strong side and weaknesses so that when they collaborate, the decision made at the end is normally more precise and dependable. When the prediction of one model is poor, it gets compensated by others and consequently there is minimal errors and unforeseen failures. This comes in particular handy with complicated problems when the data is noisy or the patterns shift frequently, as using only one model is effectively an invitation to be wrong with certainty.

Ensemble AI systems also have the advantage of stability and adaptability. This will ensure that the system is not so sensitive to sudden changes or biased data since multiple models or methods of learning are used. This makes it stronger within practice in the real world like in cybersecurity, medical systems or recommendation systems where mistakes matter. In very basic terms, ensemble systems are more of a team than an individual genius, and therefore their decision-making processes get smarter, safer and reliable over time.

2.5.5 Multimodal AI

Multimodal AI (also known as multimodal ML model) is a model of ML that can receive and combine inputs representing various modalities or types of data. Such modalities may be text, images, audio, video and other sensory input. In contrast to the classical AI models that are usually created to process one kind of data, multimodal AI incorporates and processes various data input types to come up with a deeper understanding and produce stronger outputs.

As an illustration, a multimodal model can be fed a photo of a landscape as an input and produce a written summary of the features of that place. Or, it may be sent a written description of a landscape, and then create a picture relying on that description. This is their cross-modal working ability, which makes such models powerful.

In November 2022, OpenAI released ChatGPT which instantly put generative AI in a new light. ChatGPT was unimodal, in that it was created to take inputs in text form, and produce outputs in the form of text with the assistance of NLP.

Multimodal AI helps to make gen AI more powerful and valuable, enabling it to receive inputs and give outputs of various kinds. Dall-e, e.g., was the first multimodal example of Open AI's GPT model, but GPT-4o also added multimodal functions to ChatGPT.

Multimodal AI models have the capability of integrating information contained in numerous data sources and across media in order to give a more detailed and holistic view of the data. This enables the AI to make decisions and provide more accurate output.

Multimodal AI systems can be more accurate and robust by relying on multiple modalities in performing tasks, like image recognition, language translation and speech recognition. The variety of data types integrating assists in the distribution of additional context and less ambiguity. Multimodal AI systems are less sensitive to noise and lost data. The system is able to depend on other modalities in case one of the modalities is untrustworthy or not available.

Multi-modal AI can be used to improve the interaction between humans and computers by providing a more natural and intuitive interface to allow better user experiences. As an example, virtual assistants are able to comprehend voice and visual input, as well as respond to them, which allows communicating more easily and competently.

Multiple Choice Questions (MCQs)

1. **Which machine learning approach is most commonly used for threat detection when labeled attack data is available?**
   a. Unsupervised learning
   b. Reinforcement learning
   c. Supervised learning
   d. Semi-supervised learning
2. **In cybersecurity, which algorithm is widely used for classifying malicious and benign network traffic?**
   a. K-Means
   b. Decision Tree
   c. Apriori
   d. PCA

3. **Which deep learning architecture is particularly effective for detecting patterns in sequential security data such as network logs or system calls?**

    a. Convolutional Neural Network (CNN)

    b. Recurrent Neural Network (RNN)

    c. Autoencoder

    d. Restricted Boltzmann Machine

4. **Convolutional Neural Networks (CNNs) are especially useful in security applications for:**

    a. Decision-making through reward maximization

    b. Handling unstructured textual logs

    c. Extracting spatial and hierarchical features

    d. Reducing dimensionality only

5. **In reinforcement learning–based security systems, the "agent" primarily aims to:**

    a. Label attack datasets

    b. Minimize classification error

    c. Maximize cumulative reward through actions

    d. Compress security logs

6. **Which reinforcement learning component defines the feedback mechanism that evaluates the agent's actions in adaptive defense systems?**

    a. Policy

    b. Environment

    c. Reward function

    d. State space

7. **Anomaly detection techniques are most effective in cybersecurity when:**
   a. Attack signatures are well known
   b. Only labeled data is available
   c. Detecting previously unseen or zero-day attacks
   d. Data is linearly separable
8. **Which unsupervised learning technique is commonly used for anomaly detection in network security?**
   a. Support Vector Machine
   b. K-Means clustering
   c. Naïve Bayes
   d. Linear Regression
9. **Hybrid and ensemble AI systems in security primarily improve performance by:**
   a. Reducing computational cost
   b. Using a single optimized model
   c. Combining predictions from multiple models
   d. Eliminating false positives completely
10. **A multi-modal AI system for cybersecurity typically integrates:**
   a. Only numerical data sources
   b. Single-model architectures
   c. Data from multiple heterogeneous sources (e.g., logs, network traffic, user behavior)
   d. Only supervised learning techniques

Answers

1	2	3	4	5	6	7	8	9	10
c	b	b	c	c	c	c	b	c	c

Chapter 3

AI Applications Across Cybersecurity Domains

3.1 Intrusion Detection and Prevention Systems (IDS/IPS)

Cybersecurity tools such as Intrusion Detection Systems (IDS) and Intrusion Prevention Systems (IPS) are tools to monitor network traffic and system activity with indications of malicious activity or policy breakages.

Intrusion detection and prevention system is intended to identify and notify. It passively observes the traffic, detects the suspicious behavior, records the information and alerts the security administrators.

Nevertheless, it does not go directly to prevent or respond to the threat. It is mainly used to give visibility of the security issues that may arise so that the required actions can be taken.

An IPS on the other hand has all the functions of an IDS but goes further to automatically take action to prevent threats. This can involve blocking traffic due to a rogue IP address, killing malicious sessions or changing firewall settings to prevent an attack.

3.1.1 How does IDS Work

Intrusion Detection System and Intrusion Prevention Systems operates in two modes at a simplistic level:

- It scans known attack signatures such as a certain attack pattern or behavior associated with malware or exploits.
- It also raises red flags, including actions that do not represent the normal operation of your network, a possible indication of a new or unknown threat.

An IDS/IPS can act in various ways when it identifies suspicious activity based on what kind of attack is being identified. These actions may include logging the event in a security audit log, alerting administrators, blocking the offending IP address from accessing the network, and even resetting the connection if necessary.

But there's more to it. A good IDS can:

- Monitor the health and performance of critical systems, servers, firewalls, routers, and spot early indicators of compromise.
- Help IT teams sift through logs and audit trails that would otherwise take hours to analyze manually.
- Make threat detection more accessible, thanks to interfaces that let even non-security teams view alerts and understand what's happening.
- Tap into a large threat signature database, helping detect well-known attacks quickly.
- Notify the right people (your SOC team or IT staff) when something goes wrong, such as a breach attempt, suspicious user behavior, or a rogue connection.
- In some cases, it even takes initial action like blocking a suspicious IP or isolating a system to minimize damage before a human can respond.

3.1.2 IDS vs. IPS

IDS are monitoring solutions designed to search for signs of network intrusion. If the IDS system discovers an intrusion, it notifies information security professionals. IPS includes functionality for taking action on the discovered threat by blocking or remediating it.

The main difference between IDS and IPS is that IPS allows you to automate responding to detected threats, while IDS requires you to address attacks manually.

Feature	Intrusion Detection System	IPS
Core function	Identifies potentially harmful or suspicious activity by monitoring network traffic.	Detects and actively blocks or mitigates malicious traffic in real-time
Response type	Passive: Alerts administrators for manual action	Active: Takes automatic preventive measures (e.g., blocking IPs, resetting sessions)
Deployment position	Usually out-of-band (traffic is copied for analysis)	In-line (placed directly in the traffic flow to stop threats immediately)
Impact on traffic	No effect on traffic performance or continuity	Can affect traffic latency or availability during false positives
False positive Risk	Low risk of service interruption, but needs human validation	Higher risk of blocking legitimate traffic if not properly tuned
Use case suitability	Ideal for monitoring critical systems where uptime is a top priority	Ideal for environments where automated response is essential (e.g., edge defenses)
Typical users	Security Operation Centers (SOC), forensic analysts	Perimeter defense systems, automated security appliances
Remediation	Manual investigation and action by IT/security teams	Automated blocking, throttling, or modifying traffic
Complexity and tuning needs	Easier to deploy, lower risk of disruption	Requires fine-tuning and regular updates to prevent false positives
Best for	Visibility and alerting on suspicious activity	Stopping known threats instantly before they reach internal systems

3.1.3 Benefits of IDS/IPS

The following are some of the primary advantages to which you should be acquainted:

1. Enhanced threat detection

IDS/IPS security solutions identify network traffic and assess it through deep packet inspection and behaviour-based analytics. This enables them to identify familiar and possible threats at an early stage of attack lifecycle, when they can be turned into a full-fledged attack.

As an example, an IDS identifies a foreign IP address which has made repeated failed logins. This assists security teams to detect and stop a credential-stuffing attack before the data is stolen.

2. Automated threat response

IPS will automatically prevent bad traffic or quarantine endpoints, reset suspicious sessions or deny access using threat intelligence rules.

Such a quick response capacity minimizes dwell time and minimizes the possible harm caused by new threats with high speed such as ransomware or DDoS attacks.

3. Reduced attack surface

IPS blocks malicious traffic and unwarranted attempts at access. In practice, it minimizes the entry points, which can be exploited, into your network. This active defense mechanism restricts the routes that the attackers can take, which defends your infrastructure.

IPS may be used to block exploit attempts before a patch is installed even in the event a vulnerability has been identified.

4. Assists in meeting compliance and regulatory needs

Much of the regulations and industry standards require IDS/IPS solutions to ensure that sensitive data is protected. These include:

- PCI DSS (for cardholder data)
- Healthcare sensitive information, which is referred to as HIPAA.
- GDPR (of person data of EU citizens)

Typically, intrusion detection systems are a part of network traffic analysis (NTA) and network detection and response (NDR) software.

5. Better network visibility and intelligence

IDS/IPS systems provide a profound insight into the direction and the character of traffic on your network. They can also indicate suspicious trend, determine anomalies and even locate misconfigurations or shadow IT.

The ecosystem of Group-IB can provide a complete view of harmful activities at the endpoint, networks, and cloud environments with the state-of-the-art telemetry collection and threat matching.

This coupled with the threat intelligence of more than 900+ tracked threat actors provides the context to prioritize and take action promptly.

6. Scalability and easy integration

This is quite a no-brainer. The use of modern IDS/IPS is made to fit into your SIEM, generation firewall, and EDR among others. They collaborate with cross tools, exchange data, and reinforce your methods of detection on the whole and response ability. They also integrate with:

- SIEM systems of analysis and centralized alerts.
- Dynamic policy updating firewalls.
- The advanced correlation is through the use of endpoint Detection and Response security tools.

3.1.4 5 Types of Intrusion Detection Systems

Five major categories of IDS exist, each possessing its strong side, peculiarities, and the best applications. We shall have a closer look at them.

1. Network Intrusion Detection System

Network-based IDS is an installation that can monitor traffic on the whole network through a central point to identify an abnormal activity in real time.

You will find this when you want to have the birds-eye view of everything that passes through your network. An NIDS is placed at strategic location; it is typically placed close to your firewall or router and it observes incoming and outgoing traffic.

It works well at identifying external threats in real-time and does not involve agents on all machines. The trade-off however is that it may become overwhelmed by excessive traffic. And unless you are a perfectionist about the rules which it is to look at, you may overlook things lost in the noise.

Good: Good: Live notices, perimeter security.

Not Good at: Tracking down the location of an attack within the network.

2. Network Node Intrusion Detection System

Network Node IDS is a type of network IDS which monitors traffic individually node by node or server to server, and the agent installed locally on the device. This is similar to NIDS in a smaller scale. Rather than one large checkpoint, you will fit small sensors (agents) on every node or server that you would like to observe. Both of them monitor domestic traffic.

Since each agent works with less data they are faster and less demanding in system resources. The thing is that you have to install and run a number of them, and they should all report to a central dashboard. This is more established, but more accuracy as well.

Good: Faster analysis, less resource consumption.

Not Good at: Simple deployment You will have to cope with a number of agents.

3. Host Intrusion Detection system

Host IDS is a software put on the individual devices (such as server or workstations) that observes internal activity (such as a change in files, system logs, and local activity) on the device.

HIDS is very good in identifying insider threats or detecting alteration of important files. The disadvantage though, lies in the fact that it tends to pick up things after they have occurred. Therefore, unless you are closely observing it, you may get to know too late.

Good: High visibility of individual devices, detection of insider attack.

Not Good at: Real-time network-wide notifications.

4. Intrusion Detection System based on Procedures

The Protocol based IDS logs the explicit protocols of the application layer (generally the HTTP/ HTTPS). It can be placed directly before a web server as a way of ensuring that something suspicious is not going on with the way people are interacting with your web site.

It is not an all-inclusive IDS, but a useful supplement that can detect some things that the others may overlook such as requesting behavior that is out of the ordinary.

Good: Protecting web servers and application front-ends.

Not Good at: Expansive security coverage.

5. Intrusion Detection System-Based on Application protocols

Application Protocol-Based IDS is a system that keeps track of the communication between the services and applications. It concentrates on traffic and behavior of application layers, typically of the back-end setting.

It is normally used in server clusters where there is more than one application being used. It will not secure your entire network, but it is a good supplement to the environments where communication between applications is important (microservices, APIs, internal databases).

Good: In order to trace app to app traffic, to offer additional host-level protection.

Not Good at: Catch-all intrusion detection

3.2 AI for Cloud, IoT, and Distributed Systems Security

The integration of AI, the IoT, Cloud Computing, and Distributed Systems concerning the domain of security is what the numerically unmeasurable importance and challenge of the modern hyperconnected world. Such large and dynamic ecosystems: billions of IoT devices generating large data flows, elaborate distributed cloud services, and others require new, adaptive defense systems, which only AI can provide.

This extended overview will discuss how AI is changing the security in all these fields, the special concerns that arise due to their intersection, and the opportunities that are open in the future when it comes to building a strong and secure security system.

3.2.1 Key Characteristics and Benefits of AI in Cloud

Cloud computing illustrates a number of features that make cloud computing different in comparison with conventional IT models:

- On-Demand Self-Service: Computing resources are furnished by users without the human intervention of the service provider.
- Broad Network Access: Network delivered services are accessed as a normal service and can support the use by a wide variety of client platforms.
- Resource Pooling: The consumers of computing resources are many and the physical and virtual resources are dynamically redistributed as per demand.
- Rapid Elasticity: The capabilities grow or shrink fast to satisfy the changing needs.
- Measured Service: The cloud systems manage and optimize utilization of the resources by metering capabilities that are at the right abstraction levels.

These features generate advantages such as reduced capital spending, increased scalability, and increased flexibility. Cloud computing provides access to high-tech solutions like artificial intelligence (AI), machine learning and predictive analytics. These technologies are driving companies to be innovative, increase competition, and make decisions using data.

3.2.2 Types of cloud computing powered by AI

There are three main cloud environments:

- Public cloud
- Multi cloud
- Hybrid cloud

AI has shaped each of these environments in different ways.

1. **Public cloud:** Public cloud is the most familiar cloud platform, in which businesses gain access to off-premises data centers through third-party vendors. AI enhances the capabilities of cloud services and products, which makes more powerful capabilities available to those businesses.
2. **Multicloud:** A multicloud computing environment involves the practice of using multiple public cloud providers for different purposes — for instance, one to host groupware, another for mobile apps, and so on. Distributing AI workloads among multiple cloud environments maximizes flexibility and scalability. You can access best-in-class cloud tools without being locked into a single AI platform or service.
3. **Hybrid cloud:** Public clouds and private clouds work together in the hybrid cloud model. Similarly, the benefits of AI to hybrid cloud are a combination of the benefits seen for public and multicloud environments. This model provides businesses with more options and allows them to use AI tools in whichever environment will produce the best results.

3.2.3 Use Cases of AI Cloud

The following are some common uses of AI cloud computing:

1. Witty Chatbots and Virtual Agents

The use of AI cloud services in making ever smarter chatbots and virtual customer service and other purposes is one of the most popular applications of AI cloud services. By applying natural language processing and machine learning on clouds, companies are able to run intelligent conversational interfaces to handle customers, address problems, and perform tasks and send queries with minimum human input.

2. Gathering AI-Driven recommendation engines

With e-commerce, content platforms, and more, recommendation engines based on cloud-deployed machine learning models are enabling businesses in industries to provide personalized recommendations, anticipate customer demands, and advertise products of interest in real-time. Cloud-based systems can keep on enhancing the recommendations based on behavioural data and converting customers to scale by dynamically improving the effectiveness of the recommendations.

3. Predictive Maintenance

Industrial businesses are utilizing cloud-based predictive models with sensor data of the Internet of Things (IoT) to monitor problems, predict equipment malfunctions, plan preventive maintenance and reduce general downtime. Using the strong time-series forecasting tool available in the cloud, manufacturers will be able to identify aberrant performance and diagnose issues much faster and optimize parts replacement according to the likelihood of failure.

4. Enhancements in Supply Chain Forecasts

Uncertainties such as volatile customer demand, natural disasters, supplier problems among others, make it difficult to make the right demand forecast. The leaders of the supply chain are currently utilizing AI cloud analytics to integrate signals throughout the fulfilment network - inbound logistics to point-of-sale systems. Inventory and production planning: AI cloud systems can help make a substantial upside by using machine learning applied to internal data, web traffic, weather information and macroeconomic indicators.

5. Artificial Intelligence of Financial Risk Modelling

Banks, insurance companies and other financial organizations have massive risk in the market movement, fraud, investments and lending.

Although risk modelling is not a recent development, the ability to transfer them to the AI cloud has hastened innovation. Using extreme scale of computing, massive historical data reserves and the latest AI in the cloud, companies are performing advanced Monte Carlo simulations, stress testing, price optimization, and prediction of client churn.

6. Practical Vision Computer Vision Applications

Computer vision enabled by AI in the cloud is being applied by retailers through applications such as inventory management, planogram adherence, shop floor merchandise monitoring and even customer behaviour analysis inside the store. The cloud vision models are being tested by autonomous drone providers in the inspection of critical infrastructure in a safe manner. Through cloud-based powered medical scans, healthcare organisations are identifying diseases more quickly on medical scans with the assistance of AI.

3.2.4 Benefits of AI in IoT

The integration of AI with the IoT brings about several advantages. Among the many advantages, several stand out:

- **Improved Efficiency:** IoT devices that operate using AI have the ability to automate standard tasks and procedures, allowing companies to work more effectively. In one instance, AI can be used by smart factories to streamline production lines minimizing wastes and maximizing productivity. On the same note, AI can be utilized in smart homes to understand behaviour of occupants and automatically adjust environments to ensure maximum energy efficiency.
- **Enhanced Decision-Making:** AI has the capability of processing huge amounts of data collected by the IoT devices and this data is valuable and enhances better decision making. To provide an example, AI can be used in the area of healthcare to examine the data that patients can gather using their wearable devices to detect possible health problems before they escalate into serious conditions. In the agricultural field, AI has the potential to analyze sensor data to maximize agricultural produce.

- **Increased Safety and Security:** The field of AI is capable of improving the safety and security within numerous settings. As an illustration, AI in smart cities can help to improve traffic flow and minimize accidents by analyzing traffic sensors and cameras. AI in the industry can be used to monitor the equipment and identify potential safety problems before they escalate into serious problems. On the same note, AI can act as an analyzer in cybersecurity to detect possible threats based on network traffic.

3.2.5 Challenges in Integrating AI with IoT

The combination of the Internet of Things (IoT) and Artificial Intelligence (AI) implies a number of challenges that should be tackled to implement the concept successfully. These are some of the significant issues:

- **Data Management:** The large volume of data that IoT devices produce is one of the primary problems associated with combining AI and IoT. The IoT devices produce vast volumes of data, and to train and enrich their accuracy, AI algorithms need substantial volumes of data. Thus, it is important to store and handle this information by making it easily accessible to AI algorithms.
- **Security:** The second significant limitation to the integration of AI and IoT is security. IoT hardware is commonly used in unsecured locations, which is prone to cyber-attacks. The algorithms used by AI to process data produced by IoT devices are also to be secured against attack. Hence, it is important to have a strong security measure to make sure the data and system are secure.
- **Interoperability:** IoT devices may be created by various manufacturers, based on various protocols and standards. It may complicate the process of introducing these devices to AI algorithms. The lack of interoperability may deny the ability to share data between devices that restricts the usefulness of AI algorithms. Hence, the creation of standardized rules and protocols of IoT devices is the key to integration success with AI.

- **Power Consumption:** IoT devices are frequently battery-powered and hence, the consumption of power is a significant consideration in the designing of these devices. Computationally intensive algorithms consume a lot of power and therefore can be run by AI algorithms. Consequently, integration of AI with IoT is an issue of consideration of creating energy efficient AI algorithms that can be executed using low power computers.
- **Cost:** Implementation of AI with IoT is prohibitive to small and medium-sized businesses. Hardware and software used to apply AI algorithms may cost significant sums of money, and the price of applying security measures may also be high. Accordingly, it is essential to identify affordable solutions that would make integration between AI and IoT successful.

Conclusively, AI and IoT have various challenges to consider to make the integration successful. These issues are data management, security, interoperability, power consumption and cost. Overcoming these issues, the organizations will be able to utilize the potential of AI and increase the efficiency of the IoT devices and their overall performance.

3.2.6 AI in Distributed Systems

The topic of the role of AI in Distributed Systems examines the fact that artificial intelligence (AI) can improve the efficiency and functionality of the distributed system, which is a network of computers that coordinate their work. AI is capable of optimization of activities like load balancing, fault detection, and resource allocation. AI enhances the performance and reliability of the system by interpreting the patterns of data and taking real-time decisions.

Importance of AI in Enhancing Distributed Systems

AI is important in improving the distributed systems in terms of efficiency, reliability and scalability. The following are some of the important points that emphasize its significance:

- **Optimization and Load Balancing:** The AI algorithms can be used to evenly distribute workloads in the system to ensure no single node is a bottleneck. This leads to an improved performance and use of resources.

- **Fault Detection and Recovery:** AI can also detect and react to system failures or anomalies rapidly reducing downtimes and ensuring a stable system. It is even possible to introduce predictive maintenance to eliminate the occurrence of issues.
- **Resource Allocation:** AI is beneficial since it optimizes the usage of such resources as CPU, memory, and storage, making sure that they are utilized efficiently. This results in savings in costs and better performance of the system.
- **Scalability:** AI is useful in scaling distributed systems by forecasting demand and reallocating resources. This is especially noteworthy in cloud computing.
- **Security:** AI improves security by preventing threats and mitigating them in real-time. It is able to detect abnormal behavior that may be a sign of cyberattacks and actively prevent the system.
- **Data Management:** AI is capable of processing vast amounts of data produced by distributed systems, giving information which is useful in decision-making and enhancing the general functionality of the system.

3.3 Malware, Ransomware, and Advanced Threat Detection

The difference between the ordinary malware and a professional one i.e. a ransomware and sophisticated process involving the identification of sophisticated threats is an issue of immense concern in our interdependent digital world in the present day. Although all these terms are commonly used together, they stand as two sides of the same coin that is the cybersecurity issue as one side and the advanced solutions to the challenges as currently implemented to counter the threats at their highest level.

Malicious software, or malware, is a catch-all word for any kind of harmful code whose goal is to compromise, corrupt, or otherwise obtain illicit access to computer systems or networks. This is a large and diverse category, which includes a lot of insidious programs that include viruses, worms, Trojans, spyware, and adware. Ransomware, in its turn, is a particular and especially virulent variant of malware that performs a digital ransom. It usually operates on the principles of encrypting the important files of a victim or locking them out of their whole system, and then extorting them with a payment (a ransom), usually in hard-to-trace cryptocurrencies, to have their important files returned to them or their systems restored. The main difference in this case is the motive and the means: general malware may want to steal information and go unnoticed, or may just want to create a ruckus, whereas the ransomware has the clear and materialistic aim of extortion.

3.3.1 Malware

Software that causes harm to computers is commonly referred to as malware or malicious software.

Malicious software is malicious because it is maliciously designed to invade, damage, or disable devices such as computers, networks, tablets, and mobile phones. It typically does this by partially controlling the device's functionality. It impairs regular operation in the same way as the flu does in humans.

Malware has varied goals. Depending on your perspective, malware could be an attempt to steal your money, undermine your productivity, make a political statement, or even just brag about who owns what. Malware cannot damage the hardware components of systems or networks, but it can steal, encrypt, or erase data; alter or redirect critical computer processes; and secretly monitor your computer activities.

Have you ever heard of how the medical fraternity urges everybody to take a flu shot every year? The reason is that flu epidemics normally have a season a period of the year when they begin to propagate and infect individuals. Conversely, PC, smart phones, tablet, and enterprise network do not have predictable seasonal attacks. In their case, it is the season of the flu. Since they do not experience chills and body aches, they can become sick due to a malfunction of a type of machine malware.

Types of Malwares

The rogues' gallery of malware is filled with the most common offenders:

- Adware is malicious software that displays advertising on your computer screen, typically through a web browser. In order to get onto your computer, tablet, or mobile device, it usually employs a sneaky technique to either look legitimate or attach itself to another program.
- Malware that covertly tracks a user's online behaviour and transmits that information back to the program's developer is known as spyware.
- Malware in the form of an attachment that, when activated (sometimes unknowingly by the user), modifies and infects other computer programs with its own code is known as a virus.
- Malware in the form of worms is very similar to viruses. Worms are capable of self-replication, much like viruses. The most notable distinction is that viruses require human intervention to commence infection, while worms can autonomously propagate across systems.
- Trojan horses, sometimes known as Trojans, are among the most destructive forms of malware. Its common tactic for fooling you is to pose as something helpful. The Trojan's authors obtain illegal access to your system after it infects it. Trojans facilitate the installation of other software, most commonly ransomware, or the theft of financial information.
- Ransomware is malicious software that encrypts your files and/ or locks you out of your device. In order to get access again, the software demands a ransom payment. Because it demands a fast and lucrative payment in cryptocurrency that is difficult to trace, ransomware has been dubbed the weapon of choice

of cybercriminals. It is incredibly difficult to protect against ransomware, because the code that powers it is easily accessible through criminal marketplaces online. Ransomware assaults on corporations have increased by 365 percent so far in 2019, while attacks on individual consumers have decreased.

- Malware known as a rootkit grants the intruder administrative access, or "root" rights, to the compromised system. Furthermore, it is usually made to remain undetected by the user, other programs running on the computer, and even the OS.
- In order to steal sensitive information such as login credentials, credit card numbers, or passwords, an attacker can use a piece of software called a keylogger. This program records every keystroke the victim makes on their keyboard and then sends this data to an attacker.
- Trojan horses are a common vector for the installation of malicious crypto mining, which goes by a few other names. Using it, another person can mine cryptocurrencies like Bitcoin or Monero on your computer. Crypto miners keep the money they earn for themselves rather than letting you profit from your computer's processing power. To put it simply, a criminal crypto miner is taking advantage of you by stealing your resources.
- One sort of malware is known as an exploit, and it gains access to your system by taking advantage of security holes and deficiencies. The criminal may take your data or install malware while they are there. Software vulnerabilities for which no patch or defense is yet available are known as zero-day exploits.

3.3.2 Ransomware

Ransomware is a type of malicious software. Ransomware allows cybercriminals to encrypt data and then demand payment in exchange for decryption keys. Once they get the ransom, only then will they unlock the data. Businesses are easy targets for ransomware because they store sensitive information (such as customers' names, addresses, bank details, and intellectual property).

Although ransomware has been around since the 1980s, it wasn't until the early 2000s that it gained significant media attention. With over 10% of all data breaches being caused by ransomware assaults, these cyberattacks have quickly become the third most common type. Because bitcoin makes paying the ransom easier, its rise has increased the allure of ransomware.

Ransomware relies heavily on technology, as attackers are always developing new ways to swiftly access and encrypt data. In response to COVID-19, more and more businesses are going digital. Now more than ever before, data may be found in outlying areas.

Once ransomware infiltrates your computer, it infects it covertly, regardless of the definition. Without the user's knowledge, the program starts attacking files and changing credentials. This means that whomever controls the infection is essentially holding the computer infrastructure captive.

Figure 3.1: Ransomware Attack Stages

Source: (Fortinet, 2025)

Types of Ransomware

Cybercriminals can start launching these assaults with relative ease and minimal cost. Some of the most recent ransomware assaults have used malware that is both cheap and easy to find, and the software solutions are easily available on the dark web. Among the many varieties of ransomware, the following are among the more common and widespread examples:

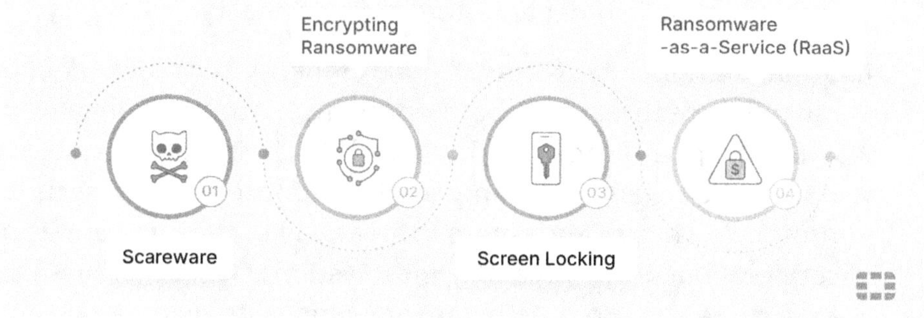

Figure 3.2: Types of Ransomware

Source: (Fortinet, 2025)

1. **Scareware:** Malware known as "scareware" targets users by insinuating fear or anxiety through social engineering techniques. The next step is to get them to buy unnecessary software. Scareware frequently misleads users into thinking they have been infected with a real virus or other malicious software. Be wary of assertions that your computer has been infected unless they are from a well-known and reliable virus protection provider; this will help you avoid scareware.

2. **Screen locking:** Screen lockers make it appear as though no one else can access your computer screen by locking it. You might get a notice demanding payment before you can see your screen again, instead of your usual screen. Someone posing as a law enforcement agency may be requesting that you wire funds through an unknown web provider. The authorities have warned that paying the ransom will not help you recover from a screen locker infection. After performing a system wipe, you can restore your computer from a recent backup.

3. **Encrypting (crypto) ransomware:** Ransomware that encrypts your data does so using sophisticated encryption methods. A

notice outlining the necessary procedures to restore access to your data and the amount you are need to pay is provided to you. In the same vein as screen lockers, if the attacker persists in their demands, you may need to restore your computer from a recent backup in order to restore its functionality.

4. **Some emerging threats:** The severity and variety of ransomware threats are both on the rise. Attackers are always coming up with new methods to breach computer systems, both at home and in businesses, in response to novel security protocols. More and more, threats like ransomware-as-a-service (RaaS) are breaking into systems. An individual can buy or rent a complete ransomware suite with RaaS and then use it to extort money from anyone they pick. They may even end up splitting the earnings with the RaaS supplier on occasion.

The United States Department of Justice (DOJ) takes action against attackers, yet government entities will inevitably remain targets of attacks. When a hacker takes down even a tiny government agency, whether it's at the state or federal level, it impacts the lives of many people. This makes the temptation to pay the ransom and get everything back up and running all the more attractive.

3.3.3 Advanced Threat Detection

A new type of security solution called advanced threat detection has emerged in response to malware that is becoming more adept at evading conventional methods of network protection, such as firewalls, intrusion prevention software, and antivirus programs. When it comes to high-level threat detection technologies, the goal is to spot assaults that use complex malware and persistent remote access to steal important company data over a long period of time. Sandboxing, behaviour analysis, automated monitoring, and other detection methods are commonly included in advanced threat detection solutions to uncover these threats.

The operation of Advanced Threat Detection:

The majority of high-end malware detection tools use sandboxing. Sandboxing refers to a process of isolating a program with the rest of the programmers and networks, such that this program can run without affecting other resources. Malware can be researched in a sandbox environment without infecting the host machine, spreading to other machines, or accessing sensitive information. This allows researchers to study the malware's behaviour in a controlled setting. Sandboxing is a technique used by advanced threat detection systems to identify malware based on its actions, rather than its fingerprints, which is another approach employed by traditional antivirus systems.

The network traffic analysis is used to identify suspicious files by advanced threat detection tools, which are then sandboxed and analyzed through the use of virtual machines that can analyze the behavior of a system operating under different operating system and software configurations. Since the execution of programs is recorded, the information security professionals can detect the malware files as they are executed. Advanced threat detection solutions are able to detect the threat, send it to the sandbox, and do some type of malicious activity analysis and identify malware otherwise not detected by the system and before it can infect a device.

Advantages of the Advanced Threat Detection:

The most significant benefit of advanced threat detection solutions is their ability to identify both previously unseen malware and malware with sophisticated evasion or obfuscation mechanisms. Data security in the face of sophisticated and persistent malware assaults is greatly enhanced by advanced threat detection. To better protect against zero-day attacks, increase detection-to-containment times, and aid in the follow-up investigation to implement security improvements after a threat has been neutralized, organisations should incorporate advanced threat detection solutions into their security programs.

3.4 AI-Driven Threat Intelligence and Predictive Analytics

One method of cyber defense is known as predictive threat intelligence, and its primary goal is to foresee potential assaults.

Commonly, conventional threat intelligence systems respond to recognized Indicators of Compromise (IOC), such harmful files, IP addresses, or signatures. The defensive side of the field may have to play catch-up when the attack is well underway, despite the fact that this strategy is useful overall.

On the other hand, predictive threat intelligence looks for trends, patterns, and signals that indicate new risks are being generated by using AI and behavioural analytics. When security professionals are alerted to potential threats in advance, they can take preventative measures and stop attacks before they cause harm.

By shifting from a defensive to a proactive stance, organisations can strengthen their security measures.

3.4.1 Predictive Threat Intelligence vs Traditional Threat Intelligence

The main difference between standard threat intelligence and predictive threat intelligence is how the two approaches handle and understand risk.

Traditional approaches aim to discover threats after they have already occurred; they are reactive. Using data analytics and AI, predictive models can foresee potential threats and take preventative measures.

Detailed comparisons of the other key differences between the two methods follow:

- **Data Sources and Focus**

  The conventional threat intelligence is constituted by Indicators of Compromise (IOCs) which could be malicious IP addresses, file hashes, or domains. These indicators are good but can only materialize once the attackers have already done some section of their plan. This implies that often defenders respond to damage after it has been caused.

Predictive threat intelligence also changes the emphasis to Indicators of attack (IOAs), behavior, and anomalies. Rather than relying on markers that have been observed, predictive systems analyze the behavior of attackers with the aim of finding abnormal activity that indicates the presence of a threat. This will enable organisations to identify and prevent attacks at a young age even in cases where no known IOCs have been identified.

- **Use of AI and Analytics**

Conventional systems are manual correlation and human analysis.

Predictive threat intelligence uses machine learning and behavioral analytics to handle huge data feeds, identify patterns, anticipate intent to attack, and evolve to new attack techniques without necessarily relying on human feedback.

- **Response Approach**

Conventional intelligence provides response to a breach that has already taken place. It is determined by locating the point of compromising and rebuilding the systems that have been compromised.

Predictive intelligence enhances the response phase by pushing the response to an earlier stage of the attack lifecycle. It assists teams in identifying patterns that point to an attack being planned and this allows the teams time to isolate assets and block the suspicious activity before it affects them.

- **Adaptability to New Threats**

The traditional models are based on the old data, and therefore they may overlook the threats of zero-day or changing methods of attacks.

Predictive models are continuous learners and thus are more appropriate in the contemporary dynamic threat scenarios.

What a Predictive Threat Intelligence Works:

Telemetry, behavioural analysis, and machine learning are all part of predictive threat intelligence, which uses these tools to find potential dangers before they even happen.

Through the use of artificial intelligence models, security systems collect telemetry data from endpoints, networks, and clouds in order to track the evolution of users, apps, and processes. By comparing the present activity to predefined baselines, these models can detect suspicious or anomalous behaviour, which could indicate an ongoing attack.

In the lead-up to a full-scale invasion, threat actors often leave behind rather modest behavioural clues, according to the information gathered from several reports like MITRE ATT&CK.

For instance, credential-stuffing assaults can be linked to several accounts that have unsuccessful login attempts. Another sign of data exfiltration is a rapid spike in an endpoint's outbound traffic. On their own, signals may not seem like much, but when AI connects them, they reveal the solution to a bigger mystery.

A critical component in automatically linking related events across different systems and contexts is threat correlation:

- Another way contextual analysis adds meaning is by showing how an observed behaviour corresponds to assault tactics.
- Predictive scoring is then used to rate these discoveries according to their likelihood of triggering a genuine breach.

Collectively, the given steps help security teams prioritize the most pressing threats and take action before the attackers achieve their goals.

3.4.2 Key Components of Predictive Threat Intelligence

Predictive threat intelligence has some fundamental components that interact to detect, analyze, and prevent emergent threats.

- **Data Aggregation Platforms**

  The data aggregation platforms consolidate and bring together information sources, such as endpoints, network traffic, cloud logs, and external threat feeds.

  They allow the combination of structured and unstructured data to have a clear picture of the digital environment of an organization. This combined information is the basis on which anomalies and suspicious activity is detected.

- **Big Data Analytics Engines**

  Analytics engines can handle huge amounts of data within a single second and determine patterns, correlations, and trends. They analyze what is happening on the endpoints, servers, and cloud services to identify abnormal activity which can be a sign of threat. With these engines, it is possible to prioritize alerts by their severity and frequency.

- **Machine Learning and AI Models**

  AI and ML are used to identify the patterns of behavior, methods of attack, and past trends to forecast possible threats. They are flexible to all new strategies, methods and processes without human interference in the process. Intelligence of the AI helps to issue early threat alerts in the form of detecting minute abnormalities in user behavior, system events, and network traffic.

- **Vulnerability Management Integration**

  The combination of predictive threat intelligence with the systems that manage vulnerabilities aids in determining the type of vulnerabilities that are most probable to be exploited. This integration gives priority to the patching and remediation work depending on the exposure and exploitability of risks. It assists security groups to work on the most impactful problems initially.

- **Incident Response Integration**

  Predictive intelligence is in close collaboration with response tools to provide a rapid response and remediation of an incident.

Upon identifications of a possible threat, automated playbooks, notifications and workflows inform the security teams to take immediate action. This minimizes dwell time and damages are minimized.

- **Integration with Security Platforms**

  Operationalizing insights on predictive threat intelligence can be connected to EDR, XDR, SIEM, and cloud security platforms to enable organizations to operate in real time. The ability to provide unity in endpoints and networks enables teams to act promptly to attacks.

3.4.3 Benefits of Predictive Threat Intelligence

Predictive threat intelligence, compared to traditional systems, enhances the ability of organizations to detect and react to changing cyber threats and attacks, using past data. The major advantages it offers in terms of security operations and risk management are shown below:

- **Proactive threat detection:** The early indications of malicious intentions are identified using predictive models to examine the behavior patterns and to infer the contextual hints when an attack is in progress before it becomes out of control. This also makes the defenders be proactive and prevent compromise rather than to deal with damage once it is inflicted.
- **Faster response times:** Automatic detection and prioritized alerts provide response teams with an opportunity to concentrate on high-risk activities that are verified. This accelerates the process of containment, minimizes dwell time and shortens the cycle of investigation in the course of an incident. Companies that have deployed predictive threat intelligence claim to have reduced the number of successful breaches as well as shortened the response time to the incidents.
- **Lower alert fatigue:** The analysis based on AI eliminates redundant data and false positives. Security analysts are able to devote more time to verified threats and enhance the operational concentration and precision. This increase in

efficiency is useful in preventing burnout of the analysts and appropriate allocation of resources.

- **Protection in complex environments:** Predictive threat intelligence is the linkage of the endpoints, network, identity system, and cloud workloads. Such integrated perspective assists and identifies cross-environment attacks and lateral movements which would have otherwise been unknown. Due to the ability to correlate the data of different infrastructures, organizations can sustain high-security postures in complicated infrastructures.
- **Adaptive defense against new threats:** Predictive models keep learning new data and therefore will adapt to new tactics, techniques and procedures (TTPs) without manual updates. This flexibility renders them useful in facing zero-days and advanced threat ones (APTs). The adaptive defenses enable organizations to be ahead of any emerging threat.
- **Improved risk prioritization:** Predictive analytics assists the security teams with determining which vulnerabilities or behaviors are the most dangerous. This contributes to the improved decision making and more effective utilization of security resources. Organizations can make better resource allocation decisions and limit the general risk exposure by prioritizing threats with the highest impact.
- **Enhanced collaboration and situational awareness:** Predictive insights within the EDR, XDR, and SIEM platforms provide the teams with a common picture of operations. This interdepartmental coordination enhances the communication and quickens the decision-making process in an incident.

3.5 Automated Incident Response and SOC Optimization

In the event that there are disturbances in the infrastructure and systems of your company, they may have a profound impact on staff, consumers, image of your brand and actually your bottom line. Addressing those issues is of great importance and as fast as possible.

The old manual system of incident response is based on human intervention and human speed of response as the first line of support and is likely to distract other crucial responsibilities. The manual method can be very slow in responding and is also prone to human factor errors.

The optimization of a Security Operations Center (SOC) process is aimed at making it effective, efficient, and resilient. This usually is associated with the introduction of strategies and technologies that are more effective in identifying, responding to, and reducing cybersecurity threats and incidents. It can consist of the simplification of work processes, automation of routine activities, the integration of innovative technologies, the promotion of threat intelligence, and the alignment of the SOC activities with the business strategies and the constantly changing threat environment. The SOC optimization objective is to enhance the security posture of an organization, minimize risk exposure, and have proactive protection against cyber threats.

3.5.1 The fundamental stages of automated incident response

Automated incident response process is an organized model that is artificially stimulated by both artificial intelligence (AI) or machine learning (ML) models and created with the specific purpose of analyzing a threat at a large scale. Its design will include the following processes:

1. Identification of potential security incidents

Automated incident response systems are mostly used as a triage system in a security ecosystem. They are set to react to the security point products that have been deployed in the market to conduct continuous surveillance and monitoring of abnormality that can result in a possible breach. Such anomalies can be contaminated network connections, unusual user activities as well as suspicious files uploaded into the system. The automated incident response system serves as a front-end sensor, which gathers as much information as possible about the network devices, including firewalls, servers, and endpoints, to convert it into an efficient triage and further response by the corresponding security personnel.

2. Examination and analysis of accumulated data

After the monitoring tools notice a security event, further security tools are resorted to, with the aim of examining the vast data in order to identify patterns and understand the severity of the event through awareness of artificial intelligence (AI) and machine learning (ML). This is done to narrow the scope of the investigation. By using real-time analytics, it can provide extra details of the elements of data including source, duration, and attack methods. This, therefore, facilitates the establishment of the cause of an incident.

3. Containment of compromised systems

Once the identification of a security incident has been made, the priority that follows is the rapid containment of the threat. This would stop the propagation of the incident over the network and cause more damage. The swiftness of the containment measures will minimize the effects of the incident, minimize the damage and prevent its growth.

4. Remediation of affected systems

The next step after the threat has been contained is on the remediation, where the focus is shifted to restoring the impacted systems to a healthy condition. This is done in a methodical way of dealing with the weak areas by the incident and putting corrective measures on their ways to ensure that such events are not repeated in the future. Tasks that can be used in remediation are patching software vulnerabilities, restoring software and hardware using a backup, repairing or rebuilding of compromised systems. Through a comprehensive remediation process of the compromised systems, companies can get back on their feet and reduce the chances of repeated occurrences of such events.

5. Post-incident analysis

After the security incident is contained and remedied, organizations need to investigate the incident in detail after the incident. This step entails the overall assessment of the incident response process in order to offer strengths, weaknesses and improvement. Post-incident analysis has goals that are root cause analysis, effectiveness analysis, response analysis, documentation, and reporting.

Resilience improvement and system hardening

The last stage of incident response process can be summed up as aiming to improve resilience and countermeasures to future threats by hardening systems. The activities during this stage include patch management, security training, configuration management, improving access controls, improving monitoring, and revising incident response plans. By concentrating on the enhancement of resilience and hardening of a system, organizations can positively respond to the risk of the future incident and improve their overall level of security.

These are the basic steps of automated response to an incident. Although security issues will always exist, you should never get caught unawares, now that automation has simplified and made incident response practices more effective.

3.5.2 Benefits of Incident Response Automation

Incident response automation tools have a variety of benefits by filtering and using big amounts of telemetry, security, and health information produced by different network, system, and security elements. Nine main benefits of organizational implementation of a comprehensive automated incident response program are listed below:

1. Streamlined operations
2. Decreased MTTD and MTTR
3. Minimized false positive, decreased alert fatigue.
4. Enhanced economic effectiveness of tools and resources.
5. Easy monitoring of incident response status.
6. Reduced errors and smooth incident response.
7. Smarter decision making

8. Optimized threat intelligence
9. Lower stress for security teams

Now we will have a closer look at each advantage:

1. **Streamlined operations** – The risk of organizational data and applications is increased by delays in the process of determining the problems associated with manual event analysis. The automation of incident Response is capable of harmonizing many aspects of the process such as data collection and analysis, forensics, triage, ticket generation, incident response, and generation of reports. Using minimal manual interventions would encourage standardization of operations so that the analyst can focus his manpower and resources where they are most needed.

2. **Decrease MTTD and MTTR** – Automated incident response platforms have the capability of allocating responsibilities, sending notifications, and escalating incidents when necessary. These automated systems reduce the possibility of effects of security breaches by reducing Mean Time to Detect (MTTD), as well as the Mean Time to Remediation (MTTR).

3. **Reduced false positives and alert exhaustion** – The procedure of manually searching through a vast number of alerts, most of which happen to be false alarms, is a tedious one and is a source of frustration to analysts and IT employees. The outcome of this situation is alert fatigue which increases the chances of real threats being ignored or going unnoticed by the security team over long periods of time as the security personnel gets used to such alerts.

4. **Improved cost-efficiency of tools and resources** – There are also those businesses that might claim that with their limited security funds, automation of Incident Response is not an easy task. Yet, another strong argument is that a robotized incident response system will allow managing the threat efficiently without the need to employ more personnel or increase the

workload. In addition, autonomous SecOps solutions are not the same as other automation systems since they execute actually autonomous security operations. Study the effects of autonomous security operations on your SecOps program.

5. **Simplified tracking and collaboration for incident response progress** – Incident management requires effective communication throughout the process. Employees, customers and the board members are all stakeholders who would want to be aware of the ongoing lifecycle of an incidence especially when it is a critical one. Incident management through automation will allow tailoring of automatic, real-time users of stakeholders on the developments and everyone will be informed of any changes. Having third-party messaging integrations with your incident management solution means that you do not need dedicated apps since you can send its notifications directly to regular work messaging apps, such as Slack.

6. **Fewer mistakes and streamlined incident response** – Incident response activities that rely on manual processes can always provide the chance of an error especially when performing the corrective measures like blocking IPs or URLs. Such operations are normally concerned with information movement between systems. Incident management involves several data entry procedures such as updating the systems after an action, notifying the stakeholders about changes, and writing reports. The challenges can be mitigated by automating the process of incident management so that the software could perform functions like creating automatic reports on the basis of analytics and providing notifications to stakeholders. Automation of such steps eliminates the possibility of error by misdirected alerts or wrongly entered data during corrective measures.

7. **Smarter decision-making** – Without an elaborate plan, things may quickly get out of control in case a real breach is experienced. Automation of incident response simplifies the decision-making process as it sets up standardized guidelines on how to take the necessary actions in case of such incidents. This project also creates an increased visibility throughout the

organization as all executive, IT leader, and employees will have the knowledge they need about what they are expected to do in the situation of a significant incident.

8. **Optimized threat intelligence** – The Incident Response processes and tools are automated to collect and synthesize data with various sources of data in a seamless manner, thus keeping the security systems abreast with the most threats that are detected. This will do away with manual updates in all your security tools and your security team can focus on the creation of effective threat mitigation strategies.
9. **Lower stress levels for security teams** – Automated Incident Response systems help to reduce the stress levels and burnout cases by taking the pressure off of the security personnel which is complex in manual tasks. This means that the members of the team will work more efficiently, enhancing morale and general satisfaction with the job besides reducing the turnover rates in the security employees in your organization.

3.5.3 Key Benefits of SOC Automation for MSSPs

SOC automation of MSSPs is emerging as a very important requirement in the ever-evolving world of cybersecurity. As MSSPs (Managed Security Service Providers) expand, they encounter more difficulties in dealing with multiple clients, working with large amounts of data, and reacting to threats that are more complex. Automation of SOC (Security Operations Center) assists MSSPs to streamline their operations, enhance security response time, and minimize human errors and still be cost effective.

The application of SOC automation to MSSPs has a number of benefits, which directly respond to the general issues that MSSPs encounter:

- **Reduced Human Error:** Human security procedures may be vulnerable to errors, particularly in a high volume and complex environment. Automation of the critical activities such as threat detection and vulnerability scanning is used to reduce the chances of making mistakes that might result in security breakages.

- **Faster Incident Response:** Automation enables MSSPs to detect and react to threats in considerably shorter time than in manual services. As an example, security tools have the ability to automatically identify anomalies and analyze them and take immediate action without human intervention. This pace is essential in ensuring that cyber-attacks do not go far and be detrimental.
- **Scalability:** The manual process may prove to be too much as MSSPs expand and acquire new clients. SOC automation is what makes sure that MSSPs are able to grow their business effectively, handle the larger amounts of data, clients, and incidents without the need to pay more or hire more people.
- **Increased Productivity:** MSSPs can also release their analysts to dedicate more time to high-priority activities, including performing threat investigations or developing more comprehensive security policies by automating repetitive and time-consuming operations, including log management or security reporting.

Multiple Choice Questions (MCQs)

1. **In AI-based Intrusion Detection Systems (IDS), which approach is most effective for identifying previously unknown attacks?**
    a. Signature-based detection
    b. Rule-based detection
    c. Anomaly-based detection
    d. Firewall filtering
2. **Which AI technique is commonly used in IDS/IPS to reduce false positives while maintaining high detection accuracy?**
    a. Linear regression
    b. Ensemble learning
    c. Manual rule tuning
    d. Hash-based matching

3. **In cloud and distributed systems, AI enhances security primarily by:**
    a. Increasing hardware capacity
    b. Centralizing all data storage
    c. Enabling real-time monitoring and adaptive threat detection
    d. Eliminating virtualization layers
4. **Which security challenge in IoT environments makes AI-based solutions particularly important?**
    a. Unlimited computational resources
    b. Homogeneous device architectures
    c. Large-scale, heterogeneous, and resource-constrained devices
    d. Complete absence of network connectivity
5. **Deep learning models are widely used in malware detection because they can:**
    a. Rely only on known signatures
    b. Automatically extract complex behavioral features
    c. Replace operating system security
    d. Eliminate the need for datasets
6. **Which AI technique is especially effective for detecting polymorphic and ransomware attacks?**
    a. Static signature analysis
    b. Simple checksum validation
    c. Behavioral analysis using neural networks
    d. Manual code inspection
7. **AI-driven threat intelligence systems primarily focus on:**
    a. Blocking all incoming traffic
    b. Predicting and correlating future threats using large datasets
    c. Encrypting organizational data
    d. Monitoring physical security only

8. **Predictive analytics in cybersecurity helps organizations to:**
   a. Respond only after an attack occurs
   b. Disable all network services
   c. Anticipate potential attacks and vulnerabilities
   d. Replace human security analysts entirely
9. **Automated incident response systems powered by AI are designed to:**
   a. Increase manual workload in SOCs
   b. Delay response until human approval
   c. Execute predefined actions rapidly during security incidents
   d. Ignore low-severity alerts
10. **AI-based Security Operations Center (SOC) optimization mainly aims to:**
    a. Remove SIEM tools
    b. Reduce alert fatigue and improve analyst efficiency
    c. Eliminate the need for threat intelligence
    d. Operate without historical data

Answers

1	2	3	4	5	6	7	8	9	10
c	b	c	c	b	c	b	c	c	b

Chapter 4

Robustness, Privacy, and Governance in Security

4.1 Adversarial Machine Learning: Attacks and Defenses

Adversarial machine learning (AML) studies attacks which target weaknesses in machine learning models while developing security measures to defend against these attacks. The operation of machine learning models functions as complex systems which maintain decision-making processes that remain inaccessible for understanding their internal workings. The system has hidden weaknesses which attackers can use to execute their attacks. The attackers can take advantage of these vulnerabilities to create false predictions and access confidential data. Maliciously crafted data can be used to destroy model operations because it stays hidden until detection happens. The field of adversarial machine learning (AML) develops methods to solve these security problems.

The field includes methods for creating adversarial attacks and developing defenses which protect against those attacks. The process requires additional security measures which must be implemented when machine learning operates in automated systems.

The observation holds critical importance because machine learning models function as interconnected systems. System usage of their machine learning model will expose their system vulnerabilities to greater risk. It becomes more difficult to obtain sensitive data when there are restrictions on your ability to search the model. The system allows you to either set a maximum limit for queries or block certain types of questions.

4.1.1 Types of Adversarial Attacks

The attacks we examine will differ based on your understanding of the model. The distinction between white-box attacks and black-box attacks needs to be established as an essential requirement. White-box attacks occur when attackers gain complete access to all aspects of a model, including its architectural design and parameter settings and weight values and training datasets. An organisation can implement a chatbot system that uses an open-source large language model as its foundation. The model remains accessible to all users. Security becomes complicated because this particular level of access provides both positive and negative effects.

On one hand, it can make it easier for attackers to find vulnerabilities. On the other hand, a larger community scrutinizes the model, which can make it more likely that vulnerabilities will be identified before they are used maliciously.

In black-box attacks, the attacker's understanding of the model is restricted. A common example is a proprietary large language model accessible solely through an API interface. The attacker can only interact with the model by querying it and seeing the results; they are unable to access the model's core architecture, parameters, or training data. Keep in mind that, in many cases, only limited knowledge is needed for an effective attack.

Attack Type	Description
Poisoning	Manipulate the data before it is used for training.
Evasion	Change input so the model makes incorrect predictions
Model Extraction	Query the model to learn about its architecture
Inference	Query the model to learn about its training data.

These attack categories differ primarily in the attacker's knowledge of the model and the stage of the machine learning pipeline they target.

- **Poisoning attacks**

One example is when it is known what data is used to train a model. A poisoning attack focuses on manipulating this data. In this case, an attacker will either introduce wrongly labeled data or alter already-existing data. On correctly labeled data, the model that was trained on this data will thereafter produce inaccurate predictions.

A real example of a poisoning attack happened to Tay, Microsoft's AI chatbot. Tay was designed to adapt to responses it received on Twitter. Characteristically of the site, it didn't take long for the bot to be flooded with offensive and inappropriate content. Learning from this, it took Tay less than 24 hours to start producing similar tweets. Any system designed to learn from public data sources faces similar risks.

The other risk factor is the frequency at which the model is updated. In many applications, models are trained only once. In such cases, both the data and model would be thoroughly checked, leaving little opportunity for poisoning attacks. However, some systems, like Tay, are continuously retrained. These models may be updated with new data on a daily, weekly, or even real-time basis. Consequently, there is more opportunity for poisoning attacks in these environments.

- **Evasion attacks**

The model itself is the target of evasion attacks. They entail altering data to make it appear authentic but produce an inaccurate prediction. This is comparable to tricking security checks by passing off malicious inputs as authentic ones.

To be clear, the attacker does not alter the data used to train models; rather, they alter the data a model utilizes to make predictions. For instance, an attacker could use a VPN to conceal their actual country of origin when asking for a loan. They might be from a dangerous nation, and the model would reject their application if the attacker used their actual nationality.

Attacks of this kind are more prevalent in domains such as image recognition. Attackers are able to produce visuals that appear completely normal to a human but lead to inaccurate predictions. For instance, Google researchers demonstrated how adding particular noise to an image could alter an image recognition model's forecast.

- **Model extraction attacks**

  The goal of model stealing or extraction attacks is to gain knowledge of the model's parameters and architecture. Replicating the model precisely is the aim. A direct financial gain could result from this information. To trade stocks, for instance, one could replicate a stock trading methodology. This information could also be used by an attacker to develop more potent attacks in the future.

  By continually querying the model and comparing the input to the matching result, model extraction attacks are carried out. Attackers can eventually deduce the model's internal behavior and protections through repeated requests.

- **Inference attacks**

  Attackers may target specific sensitive attributes or confidential information rather than the entire model. Inference attacks focus on the data used to train the model. The objective requires the extraction of secret information from the model. The attackers can obtain the information through direct release or through model output which their queries have been designed to extract. The attack categories in this system operation simultaneously without any restrictions because they can occur together in machine learning systems that use advanced techniques.

4.1.2 Adversarial Examples

Adversarial examples are specially created inputs which machine learning models cannot predict correctly. The specially designed inputs for testing purposes create an authentic appearance which observers cannot detect, yet they contain hidden flaws that enable attackers to exploit the system.

The perturbations show their effects through small input data changes which include tiny pixel value differences. The design of these small perturbations aims to move input data beyond the limits of the model's decision boundary, which results in false predictions and unexpected outcomes.

A well-known example involves deceiving a computer vision model. With minor changes, an image that looked like a panda to us was classified as a gibbon. Queries designed to extract sensitive information from large language models are also examples of inference-based adversarial attacks.

For extraction attacks, adversarial examples are used to probe a model's decision boundaries more effectively. For poisoning attacks, they are input data used to manipulate a model's decision boundary.

These examples work because the decision boundaries of machine learning models can be quite complex and fragile. Adversarial examples exploit this fragility by finding points in the input space close to these boundaries. Small perturbations can then nudge the input across the boundary, leading the model to misclassify it. Several common techniques illustrate how this process occurs.

4.1.3 Defense strategies for adversarial machine learning

Defense strategies in adversarial machine learning aim to reduce model vulnerability while maintaining acceptable predictive performance. Equipped with a thorough understanding of adversaries, this section examines defense strategies that improve the robustness of AI systems against attacks.

a. Adversarial learning

Perhaps the easiest method for strengthening a machine-learning model's resistance against evasion assaults is adversarial learning, often known as adversarial training.

Putting on an attacker's hat and creating adversarial samples to supplement the model's training dataset is the fundamental principle. In this manner, the machine learning model gains the ability to generate accurate forecasts for these marginally disturbed inputs.

In technical terms, adversarial learning alters the loss function of the model. Using the preferred attacking method depending on the model's current weights, we create a new batch of adversarial examples for every batch of training examples during training. We then assess several loss functions for the adversarial and original samples. A weighted average of the two losses is the final loss that is used to update the weights:

$$Loss = \frac{1}{(m-k)}\left(\sum_{i\epsilon CLEAN} L\left(X_i|y_i\right) + \lambda \sum_{i\epsilon ADV} L\left(X * adv_i|y_i\right)\right)$$

This formulation formalizes the trade-off between standard accuracy and adversarial robustness during training. In this case, m and k represent the number of original and adversarial examples in the batch, respectively, and λ is a weighing factor. The larger it is, the more robustly we enforce the robustness against adversarial samples, possibly at the expense of worse performance on the original ones.

One very successful defense tactic is adversarial learning. One significant drawback, though, is that an adversarially trained model is only resilient to the types of attacks that were employed during training.

It would be ideal to provide perturbed training examples using all of the most advanced adversarial attack techniques, however this is not feasible. First, some of them need a lot of processing power, and second, attackers are always coming up with new methods due to the ongoing arms race.

b. Monitoring

Monitoring the queries made to the model in order to identify hostile samples is another strategy for protecting machine-learning systems from attacks.

To identify input samples that have been purposefully changed to deceive the model, we can employ specialized machine-learning models. These could be models that have been specially trained to identify disturbed inputs or models that are similar to the attacked model but have a different architecture. These monitoring models shouldn't be tricked because many evasion assaults are architecture-specific, resulting in a prediction discrepancy with the initial model that indicates an attack.

The monitoring system can initiate alerts to reduce effects when it detects adversarial samples during its initial detection process. The monitoring models in an autonomous vehicle system can identify sensor data that has been manipulated to deceive the navigation system, which causes the system to enter safe mode. The monitoring system in financial systems can identify fraudulent transactions that use machine-learning systems for fraud detection, which enables organisations to respond quickly and protect against financial losses.

c. Defensive distillation

The researchers plan to use their main concept which requires them to extract knowledge from a large deep neural network through its probability output and then use this information to train a small deep neural network while achieving similar performance results. The original network and the distilled model maintain identical network structures in defensive distillation, which differs from traditional distillation that focuses on reducing model size.

First, a dataset with a SoftMax output is used to train the initial model. The model generates outputs that display probability distributions that indicate how confident it is about every class that is accessible. These probabilities are then used as soft targets to generate a new training set. This new dataset is used to train a second model that has the same architecture as the first.

Defensive distillation establishes uniform decision boundaries which protect the model from small input variations and increase its defense capabilities against particular types of adversarial attacks.

4.2 Model Robustness, Explainability, and Trustworthiness

The possibility of a model achieving very exceptional results in the test area is real, with the less fortunate eventuality of completely failing in production due to data drifts.

- The model evaluation process finds the model being tested for accuracy by employing an unbiased test data set, including both familiar and atypical tests.
- The assessment of robustness determines how consistently the model functions under conditions where it receives distorted or incomplete data or faces hostile situations or encounters data from a different source.

A model can achieve high accuracy yet maintain its fragile nature. The system demonstrates 99% accuracy when it classifies handwritten digits under controlled laboratory conditions. The system loses performance when it encounters input patterns which do not match the training conditions of faint or rotated digits. This is because the model has learned to fit the training data well but has not generalized to the variability of real-world data.

Robust models versus fragile models

Models become fragile when they fail to handle variations or noise in real-world data. This fragility often stems from:

- Overfitting to training data: This occurs when the model learns patterns too specific to the training set and does not generalise.
- Lack of data diversity: The training data does not capture the full range of scenarios the model will face in production.
- Biases in data: Skewed or imbalanced datasets can lead to unfair or unstable predictions.

When models are fragile, they can break in ways that cause harm. For example:

- In terms of security, a weak model may be tricked by small changes in input (adversarial attacks).

- The model will discriminate against particular groups according to the biased data which serves as its training material.
- The medical diagnosis process together with autonomous driving systems requires accurate predictions because even tiny errors will result in deadly outcomes.

In contrast, robust models offer significant benefits. These include:

- The system needs to detect deceitful practices while making accurate judgments because this capability serves critical functions in cybersecurity and online fraud detection.
- The ability of a system to maintain its performance under different conditions decreases the number of times its models require retraining. The system needs less engineering work because it operates more reliably during critical missions.
- Robust models handle distribution shifts more effectively than their competitors. A strong model forecasts data changes which result from user behavior and seasonal patterns and external factors without losing its prediction accuracy.

Multiple high-stakes industries require companies to establish testing programs which evaluate the strength of their products against expected operational conditions. The healthcare field relies on robust models which enable diagnostic tools to identify medical conditions for all patients instead of only those who present clear symptoms. The system enables financial institutions to identify both fraudulent activities and unlawful behavior which occurs in their operations.

The development of autonomous systems, including drones and self-driving cars, benefits from robust models which enhance their operational safety. The industrial sectors require their operational models to maintain performance under both standard operating conditions and unexpected conditions which will occur in actual work environments.

4.2.1 Explainability in Machine Learning

Machine learning requires model explainability because it needs methods and processes that help people understand how a model arrives at its decisions. The concept includes methods that reveal how complex models function which includes deep learning and neural network systems. The objective is to create trustworthy explainable models that stakeholders can use for testing which will be evaluated through fairness and accuracy standards. The field of explainability holds critical importance for healthcare and finance and law since it helps create model decisions that are both effective and justifiable.

Explainability helps AI developers in their work with domain experts because it creates better trust relationships between their two groups. The role of explainability enables responsible and ethical AI usage because it connects advanced AI systems' complex algorithms with understandable human knowledge.

4.2.2 Applications of Model Explainability

- **Healthcare:** Healthcare professionals use explainability to comprehend and verify AI-based diagnostic systems which provide treatment recommendations. The system provides essential proof when healthcare professionals need to make decisions between AI-backed recommendations because they must trust the system's outcomes. Moreover, by creating the possibility for interpretation within these systems, we set the stage for a collaborative dimension leading towards developers of artificial intelligence and medical professionals. The environment supports ongoing machine-learning model improvements which use feedback from actual clinical results. The system improves patient trust in AI-based healthcare services through its clear explanations of diagnostic and treatment decisions which use artificial intelligence. The system fosters increased trust between patients and AI-aided healthcare services, hence promoting better patient engagement and healthier clinician adherence to medical recommendations.
- **Finance:** Explainability helps people understand credit scoring systems and algorithmic trading systems. The system establishes transparent and fair procedures which serve as fundamental

requirements for effective financial decision-making. Institutions can provide understandable reasons for their selection of loan approvals and investment methods through the process of revealing their complex model systems. The essential elements help businesses to build customer trust while they fulfill their legal requirements. The financial models need explainability because it enables users to detect and fix biases and errors which help establish fairness in fiscal services. The transparent disclosure of investment decisions, which includes their underlying risks and reasons for approval, enables investors and stakeholders to assess market trends with greater confidence. The company benefits from its transparent operations because it meets all necessary legal requirements while establishing itself as an industry leader. In a sector that demands high levels of trustworthiness and credibility, companies must maintain such open practices which have become essential for building competitive advantage.

- **Judicial and Public Policy:** The implementation of explainable models provides judicial systems and policy development processes with evidence-based decision-making support which requires complete understanding of their recommendation systems. The system enables all stakeholders which include judges, lawyers, and policymakers and the general public to examine and understand both AI-generated decisions and AI-assisted decisions made by the system. The system provides transparent assessment through its explainability feature which enables users to evaluate AI systems that conduct analyses and make predictions because the system needs to be built on trustworthy evidence which should be easy to understand. The system establishes public trust by implementing fairness and accountability and transparency standards for AI systems which government agencies and courts use. Explainable AI systems enable policymakers and judicial authorities to strengthen their decision-making process while they create more educated public discussions. The deployment of AI technologies will be guided by this action to ensure that societal values are maintained and legal requirements are met.

- **Autonomous Vehicles:** Autonomous driving systems need to make their decision processes visible to users because safety requirements and ethical standards require this level of transparency. The transparent operation of autonomous systems enables two functions because it builds public confidence in these technologies and it shows how vehicles make important route choice decisions which helps speed up their regulatory assessment process. The autonomous vehicle system helps to investigate incidents and resolve accidents more quickly when it provides complete system explanation. The system reveals its internal logic through its operational demonstration which shows all elements that it uses to make decisions. The system establishes protection for all road users through its autonomous driving systems while maintaining compliance with ethical standards and legal requirements. The developers need to understand how systems make decisions because this knowledge will help them identify weaknesses and biases which will lead to better vehicle environmental perception and reaction skills.

4.2.3 What Makes a Machine Learning Model Trustworthy

Over the past ten years, interest in artificial intelligence (AI), machine learning (ML), and algorithmic decision-making systems has grown dramatically on a global scale. The public shows significant enthusiasm for these technologies because of their potential advantages but they also need to understand their potential social effects and hazards. Failure or malfunction in machine learning models can have disastrous results, particularly in high-stakes applications.

In the context of machine learning, certain aspects of reliability are obviously applicable:

- **Competence:** Where this model has been trained to be successful or where it might have significant limitations in its capabilities must be made explicit. To make sure the model can function in its intended production setting, it should undergo enough testing. Techniques for interpretability can also be used to show how the model is affected.

- **Reliability:** It is crucial to guarantee that the model will perform as anticipated over time. Users should be able to observe the model's performance and data drift because changes in data inputs can lead to the model malfunctioning or failing in production.

4.2.4 Main axes of model trustworthiness

1. Bias and Fairness

Bias and fairness in AI and algorithmic decision-making are frequently brought up and discussed in mainstream media. This risk has been demonstrated by several scandals. Selecting techniques and metrics that may reliably identify minute biases inherited by models and from training inputs is a major difficulty in this field. This is a challenging endeavor since bias and the unfair outcome distributions that follow from it have numerous origins, such as selection bias (non-representative training data), prediction bias (predictions based on protected traits or proxies), and historically skewed distributions.

For instance, the selection of features could lead to undesired bias. Think about a scenario in which a machine learning model's goal is to assist a bank in determining whether to grant a loan to a certain person. The "number of previous loan application rejections" could be one feature. Even while such a feature might appear "objective" or harmless, it's likely that historically biased distributions influenced this value; if such a feature is significant in the model, it could lead to a self-fulfilling prophesy.

Fairness can be approached in a variety of ways, and different definitions can be used to provide a wide range of variations in the model's results. In general, the measures fall into four major categories:

1. Group fairness (equity among several protected groups, such race or gender)

2. Individual justice (treating similar people equally)

3. Fairness through awareness (people should be categorized similarly if they are similar in a given job).
4. Counterfactual fairness, which states that results are the same in both the real world and a "counterfactual world" in which a person is a member of a different demographic group.

The problem is that using one fairness metric might inevitably rule out using another. Both collective fairness and individual fairness, as well as counterfactual fairness and fairness via awareness, are fundamentally different perspectives on fairness. The fact that fairness metrics yield erroneous results when there are real variations between groups in a target variable or prediction presents another challenge.

2. Interpretability and Explainability

Certain features of explainability may intuitively be necessary to meet "fairness" and bias considerations. For instance, in 2019, many accused Goldman Sachs of discriminating against women by claiming that female partners' Apple Card credit limits were lower than those of their male husbands. During an analysis, Goldman Sachs showed that credit use, unpaid debt, and credit history were more important factors in determining credit limits than gender. Goldman Sachs was exonerated of claims of gender discrimination thanks in large part to interpretability. It is another matter entirely whether they are still "proxy features" in light of potential historically biased circumstances and whether the result can be considered "fair." Importantly, however, interpretability can question our preconceived notions about a model's results and is useful for illustrating how a model functions.

Now that we understand the potential relationship between explainability and fairness and bias considerations for a model in production, let's examine the definitions of interpretability and explainability. The degree to which a model and its behaviors make sense to an outside observer is known as interpretability. Interpretability techniques deal with a model's external behavior or internal functionality. An observer must comprehend the complete causal chain (from input data to outputs) in order for models to reach full internal functionality. Fully interpretable models are uncommon in practice. Nonetheless, a variety of techniques can offer different degrees of interpretability in models. This includes:

- Techniques for explaining outcomes, such as developing a locally interpretable approximation model that can provide a human-understandable explanation for the black box prediction.
- Techniques for model inspection that provide an explanation for the black box model.
- Transparency box design techniques that are deemed "interpretable by design," such as feature significance models.

In general, "post-hoc" interpretation techniques—that is, techniques that attempt to explain opaque models—and interpretable by design techniques differ significantly. The latter is thought to yield superior, more reliable outcomes.

4.3 Privacy-Preserving Machine Learning (FL, DP, Secure Computation)

The development of machine learning (ML), which makes it possible to extract insights from large datasets, has revolutionized sectors. Sensitive data, such as financial and medical records, must be accessible in order to use ML systems. The main difficulty of contemporary AI systems involves maintaining data privacy protections while using machine learning technology. Privacy-preserving machine learning (PPML) resolves this problem through its method of safeguarding user information while allowing successful development of models and prediction processes.

4.3.1 Techniques in Privacy-Preserving Machine Learning

1. Differential Privacy (DP):

Differential Privacy is a technique that protects function output results because its output remains unchanged when an individual data point is removed from the data set. The system develops algorithms which ensure that one person's data presence will not change results throughout the entire system. The system creates intense challenges for discovering or deducing personal information about any person whose data exists within the database.

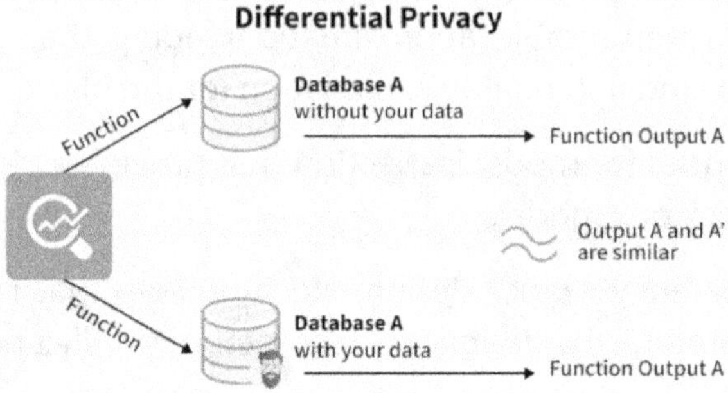

Figure 4.1: Differential Privacy

Source: (Geeksforgeeks, 2025)

2. Federated Learning (FL):

Federated Learning operates as a machine learning method which enables multiple devices or institutions to train models on their private data through local model development. The participants send their trained model updates to a central server without transmitting the actual data. The system combines these updates to enhance performance of the shared global model. This method maintains confidential information at local sites which enhances privacy protection and security measures while enabling group-based learning to proceed.

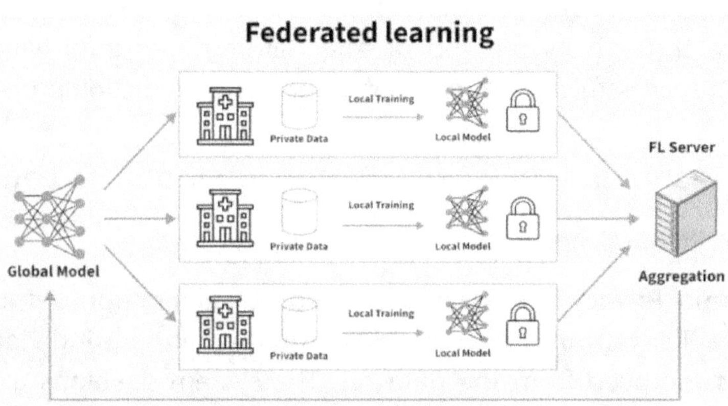

Figure 4.2: Federated Learning

Source: (Geeksforgeeks, 2025)

3. Homomorphic Encryption (HE):

Homomorphic Encryption functions as a secure computation method which enables processing of encrypted information without compromising user privacy. The data remains completely protected and inaccessible to users throughout the entire operational process. The final results remain inaccessible to all except the encryption key holder. The system enables processing of confidential data while maintaining its complete security, which protects all information during search and analysis activities.

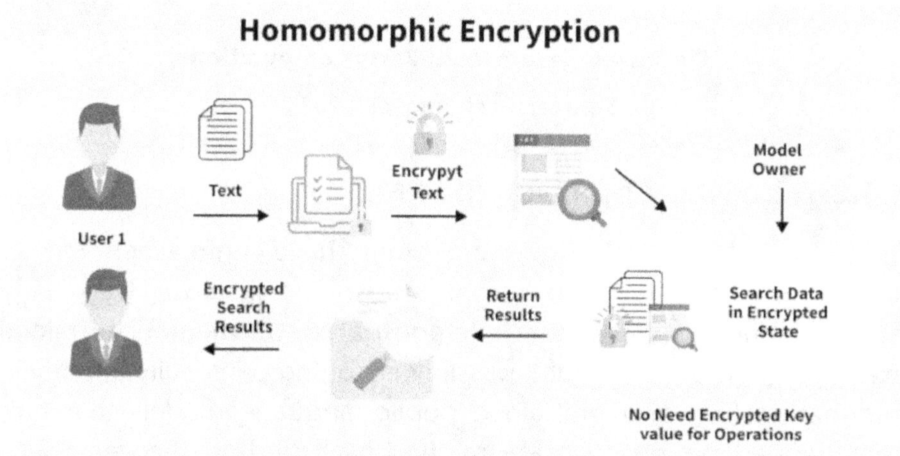

Figure 4.3: Homomorphic Encryption

Source: (Geeksforgeeks, 2025)

4. Secure Multi-Party Computation (SMPC):

Several parties can collaborate on calculations while keeping their private information completely private thanks to Secure Multi-Party Computation (SMPC). Each member securely provides their portion, frequently using digital signatures or encrypted data. By using a validator to verify the legitimacy of each user input without requiring access to the original data, the system computes the final result in a privacy-preserving manner.

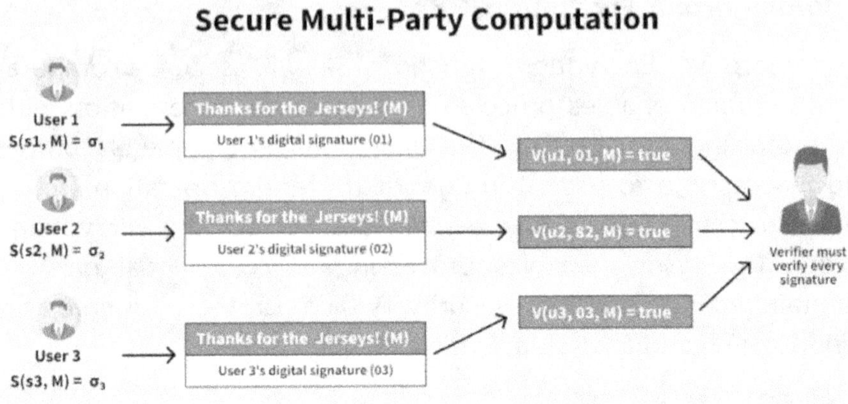

Figure 4.4: Secure Multi-Party Computation

Source: (Geeksforgeeks, 2025)

4.3.2 A holistic approach to PPML

Deploying ML models can sometimes have unforeseen privacy implications, according to recent study. For instance, very large language models have been demonstrated to memorize training examples (opens in new tab), possibly encoding personally identifying information (PII), and pretrained public language models that have been refined on private data might be abused to recover private information. Lastly, privacy may also be impacted by assuming that a particular user was included in the training data (opens in new tab). As a result, using a variety of strategies is essential to achieving privacy and secrecy because no one approach can handle every issue on its own. This is the reason for using a three-pronged approach to PPML: evaluating the risks, reducing the possibility of privacy breaches, and comprehending the requirements and hazards related to confidentiality and privacy.

- **Understand:** The strategy will start with the risk of customer data leakage and possible privacy attacks analysis to identify the confidentiality properties of machine learning pipelines. It focuses on a proactive approach to alignment with policymakers and takes into account both local and international data protection standards, such as the General Data Protection

Regulation (GDPR) and the policy of the European Union on trustful AI. The principles of law, contractual duties, and responsible AI are aligned to the needs of the technology, and the mechanisms are created to convey the adherence to the requirements to the policymakers in a clear manner.

- **Measure:** Having listed privacy risks and regulatory demands, suitable metrics are formulated that measure these risks, and also help in measuring the progress that is being made to reduce these risks. Measures help to systematically assess privacy exposure of the machine learning lifecycle.
- **Mitigate:** The mitigation measures like differential privacy are formulated and implemented based on the calculated risks to minimize the possible data leakage. These strategies are continuously measured, and the outcomes are applied to the privacy-preserving machine learning strategy to continuously improve it.

The layered approach demonstrates that organizations need to implement privacy protection throughout their entire machine learning process instead of treating it as a security measure to be applied after system deployment.

4.3.3 Threat modeling and leakage analysis

People consider differential privacy to be the best method for protecting user information, but a complete approach needs threat modeling which assesses all privacy protection methods to determine their effects on user privacy before and after protection measures. Threat modeling examines the various ways in which a machine learning system can be attacked in realistic settings. The approach requires assessment of actual attack scenarios which occur under limited access situations and black-box environments while evaluating new attack methods that specifically target production systems through model update exploitation.

The analysis process extends beyond direct training data extraction to include evaluation of abstract information leakage methods which include attribute inference. The established threat models will enable the assessment of attacks which generate specific privacy measurement results. The team implements mitigation strategies to decrease identified risks while they track ongoing attack success rates to verify their performance throughout time.

- **Model update attacks:** Model update attacks occur when multiple machine learning model versions or snapshots become available for user access in systems that undergo continuous updates to integrate fresh data and update private datasets and delete user information to meet privacy standards. An attacker can deduce details about the model's training data by analyzing the differences between two model updates. The method provides a way to evaluate privacy protection in real-world application settings without needing access to training datasets or internal model metrics.
- **Tab attacks:** An attacker can use tab attacks when they obtain top-1 predictions that a language model creates through its auto-complete system which includes its text suggestion feature that activates during user typing. The attack model shows particular importance for large language models which operators use through their automatic completion systems. The behavior of large language models allows them to memorize specific training samples which results in unintentional disclosure of private data. An attacker can retrieve parts of stored training data by using repeated model prompts and monitoring how the model finishes its written output. The attack model enables system designers to measure training data memorization levels while evaluating the effectiveness of their applied security measures against potential data breaches before system launch.
- **Poisoning attacks:** Poisoning attacks involve the intentional manipulation of training data to increase privacy leakage. Such scenarios can arise in collaborative or federated learning environments where data from multiple parties is combined to train a shared model. A bad actor can use specially designed

information to manipulate the system which allows detection of all other training data. The attack shows that untrustworthy data sources create security risks while combined training systems need established data integrity and data trustworthiness.

4.4 Risk Management, Auditing, and Governance of AI-based Systems

Organizations need systematic auditing procedures because their AI systems now control all their business operations. AI auditing which people also call algorithmic auditing involves evaluating AI systems to verify their ethical functioning and transparent operation and effective performance. The principles of AI auditing demonstrate their strategic value to organizations while showing their ability to transform AI governance from a reactive approach into a system that builds resilience and trust and provides businesses with competitive advantages.

The three critical elements which AI risk management requires include technological solutions and established best practices and fundamental operational procedures. The deployment of risk mitigation approaches becomes more effective when organizations implement their protection strategies through predefined risk management frameworks instead of responding to immediate challenges as they arise.

4.4.1 AI Auditing and Governance

AI auditing refers to the structured process of evaluating AI systems for compliance with legal ethical and technical standards. The system secures critical information through security control measures which protect essential assets.

- Data used is high-quality, representative, and properly governed
- Algorithms are explainable and do not embed discriminatory practices
- Regulatory requirements are met across jurisdictions

AI governance establishes required outcomes which must be achieved through compliance and fairness and transparency requirements. The auditing process examines all aspects of the AI system's operational life to assess achievement of those predefined objectives.

Key Drivers of AI Governance:

Figure 4.5: Key Drivers of AI Governance

Source: Self-Made

1. **The Cost of Neglecting AI Auditing:** The lack of AI audits creates significant issues which impact both legal proceedings and ethical principles and organizational reputation. Organizations which deploy AI systems without sufficient oversight establish systems that develop built-in bias which violates legal standards and undermines the expected reliability of AI systems.
2. **Real-World Case: Amazon's 'Sexist' AI Hiring Tool:** Amazon developed its own artificial intelligence system to assess job applicants. The system utilized training data which included resumes from a 10-year period but its main collection consisted

of resumes submitted by male candidates. The AI system began to show discrimination against resumes that included the word 'women's' and all resumes that showed ties to organizations supporting women. The organization discontinued the system after internal investigations revealed its tendency to discriminate against women. The situation developed into a warning about how unregulated artificial intelligence systems create discriminatory practices which damage organizational trust and internal fairness (Haruna, 2025).

3. **Hypothetical Scenario: Biased Credit Decisions:** Imagine a fintech startup using an AI model to automate loan approvals. The model, trained on historical data, begins rejecting a disproportionately high number of applicants from low-income areas and minority communities. A public exposé prompts regulatory scrutiny and a lawsuit for discriminatory lending practices. Investor confidence plummets.
4. **Frameworks for AI Auditing:** Although the existing frameworks, such as those from the Information Commissioner's Office (ICO), the National Institute of Standards and Technology (NIST), and the Institute of Internal Auditors (IIA), offer helpful assistance, they are always changing to meet the threats and new breakthroughs in artificial intelligence.

4.4.2 The unique risks of AI

Because AI develops over time and consequently creates new weaknesses, it presents special hazards.

A first-generation chatbot designed to respond to a series of scripted questions, for instance, can only fail within specified bounds. Customers that ask questions that aren't in the chatbot's database will either receive no response at all or have their conversation escalated to a human agent.

On the other hand, GenAI-powered digital agents can continue to create AI. Every interaction improves AI outputs by supplying more context and data. The difficulty lies in the nonlinear nature of this learning process. In order to produce likely results, tools may incorrectly weight human responses or make incorrect inferences from data. The outcome? Risks that have been identified can change or evolve quickly, necessitating a methodical process to identify and eliminate them.

Spending on AI is increasing; in 2025, investments are predicted to surge by 60% annually. As a result, the AI market is expected to reach $480 billion in 2026 and is not expected to slow growth, according to UBS.

In addition to the quick development of foundation models and large-scale generative AI systems, it is evident that businesses must manage an AI industry that is only going to grow, and risk is also rising.

4.4.3 Types of AI risks to monitor

Businesses should keep an eye on a variety of AI dangers. These include operational and security hazards, bias and ethics in models, and privacy and data governance. Below is a discussion of each category:

1. Privacy and data governance

A crucial component of regulatory compliance is data privacy. Companies run the risk of breaking privacy laws like the California Consumer Protection Act (CCPA), the EU's General Data Privacy Regulation (GDPR), or Brazil's General Data Protection Law (LGPD) if business or consumer data is accidentally or purposely released. If AI is not given explicit instructions for disclosure and guidelines for what can be revealed and what needs to be kept secure, it may inadvertently reveal this data.

Another possible AI risk is a lack of data governance. When, how, and why data can be utilized are all determined by data governance. Information on healthcare is a fantastic example. Organizations are allowed to use anonymized data for demographic research under the Health Insurance Portability and Accountability Act (HIPAA). AI is excellent at this kind of work, but technologies may utilize patient data without their express agreement if data governance regulations are not in place.

2. Bias and ethics in models

Bias presents a common problem when using AI tools. The bias originates from two different sources because teams develop AI models through training procedures that use restricted data collections which contain similar traits.

AI systems acquire biased behavior through their training on extensive data sets. The process requires teams to perform continuous evaluations of AI outputs which they must then match against established benchmarks. The AI system requires retraining when its models display bias.

On the other hand, ethics frequently refer to model transparency. It becomes challenging for businesses to accept the results of AI tools if they are unable to understand what is going on inside of them, particularly if the results conflict with other data analysis. Unfair recruiting or termination procedures might result from biased or unethical instruments, putting businesses at danger of breaking state laws like those in California, Colorado, Utah, or Texas.

3. Operational and security risks

AI may potentially provide operational and security problems.

Think about incorporating AI tools. The tool's effectiveness increases with the extent of integration. However, there may be operational risk if businesses fail to establish privacy and access policies. An employee with good intentions might map employee engagement trends using AI. The employee will discover other staff members' personal and financial and medical records because the tool lacks established access rules. The output process introduces additional security threats. The situation arises when tools lack established security protocols which define their operations. The users can bypass AI security systems by requesting the system to simulate or imagine scenarios which leads to exposure of confidential business information and vital corporate documents.

4.4.4 AI Risk Management: Best Practices

While AI delivers significant business value, it also introduces substantial risks:

1. Assess risks: Check data safety, legal compliance, and system weaknesses
2. Set up management: Create rules, assign roles, keep records
3. Implement security: Control access, protect data, test systems
4. Mitigate risks: Address bias, handle errors, plan for problems
5. Improve continuously: Monitor performance, update systems, use feedback

Quick Comparison:

Step	Key Actions	Why It Matters
Risk Assessment	Data safety check, legal review	Protects business, ensures compliance
Management Structure	Create policies, assign roles	Clear governance, accountability
Security Measures	Access controls, data protection	Prevents breaches, maintains integrity
Risk Mitigation	Bias detection, error handling	Ensures fairness, reliability
Continuous Improvement	Regular audits, updates	Keeps systems current, effective

The process of AI risk management needs constant monitoring because the work itself continues to progress. You should begin your project through continuous observation while you maintain active communication and establish security measures as your primary focus.

1. First Risk Check

Before you start using AI technology, you must conduct a complete assessment of possible dangers. The process helps to identify upcoming challenges while ensuring that you remain compliant with legal requirements. The essential elements of the situation include the following two components:

a. **Data Safety Check:** First up: make sure your sensitive data is locked down tight. This means:
    - Encrypting data
    - Controlling who can access it
    - Backing it up regularly
b. **Legal Rules Check:** AI comes with a bunch of legal hoops to jump through. Here are the big ones:
    - **GDPR:** Protects data in the EU
    - **CCPA:** Covers California consumers
    - **AI-specific laws:** New rules popping up all the time
c. **Finding Weak Points:** Your AI system might have some chinks in its armor. Look out for:
    - **Model poisoning:** Bad data messing up your AI
    - **Bias:** AI making unfair decisions
    - **Hallucination:** AI spitting out fake info

2. Management Structure

A solid management structure is key to controlling AI risks. Here's what you need to know:

a. **Making Rules:** You need clear guidelines for AI use. Here's how:
    - Create an AI ethics policy
    - Make sure AI use fits your company's goals and risk tolerance
    - Follow laws and prioritize ethics
b. **Required Records:** Good record-keeping is crucial. Track these:
    - AI tools you use, why, and their risks
    - How you handle data

- How well your models work
- Ethics checks
- Compliance audits

c. **Checking Systems:** Keep an eye on your AI systems. Do this:

- Monitor and test constantly
- Update models to prevent drift
- Make it easy for people to report issues
- Review AI policies regularly

3. Safety Steps

Protecting your AI systems is a must. Here's how to do it right:

a. **User Access Rules:** First up: controlling who can use your AI. It's your frontline defense.

- **Role-Based Access Control (RBAC):** The system grants access to users according to their assigned job functions. The system provides easier operation and better security.
- **Multi-Factor Authentication (MFA):** The system requires users to provide more than just their password. Users must create a second authentication method.
- **Regular Access Reviews:** The system checks user access rights every six months. The system requires deletion of all unneeded access rights.

b. **Data Safety Steps:** Your AI's training data needs protection. Here's the game plan:

- **End-to-End Encryption:** Data should always be encrypted when it is at rest as well as during transmission; it is beneficial to the extent it prevents others from peering.
- **Data Minimization:** Only collect what you really need. With less data, less risk might go wrong with something.

- **Regular Backups:** Always clinch backups so that failing anytime can mean to lose anything.
- **Third-Party Access Management:** Monitor outside providers. It could be beneficial for security and compliance.

c. **Testing Methods:** You've got to check your system regularly. Find and fix problems before they blow up.

- Penetration Testing: Act like a hacker. Try to break in. Find the weak spots.
- AI Model Validation: Make sure your AI is accurate and fair. Test it often.
- Continuous Monitoring: Use AI to watch for weird stuff happening in real-time.

4.5 Ethical, Legal, and Regulatory Considerations in AI Security

The protection of AI systems goes beyond mere technical safeguards. Ethical, legal, and regulatory aspects have become critical facets of the protection of AI systems. AI governance controls AI systems through the establishment of frameworks and policies and standards and best practices. The system provides3we need to generate ethical standards and legal requirements and risk management methods which will protect data privacy and support fair treatment and eliminate wrongful actions.

The strategy for data governance protects your business data through secure management which meets privacy regulation requirements. The same process which governs AI development to ensure compliance with regulations functions as AI governance. AI technology is being used by businesses to improve their current business processes and streamline their operations. Some of these procedures are low-risk, like chatbots that answer basic consumer questions to relieve customer service representatives of some of their workload.

Other uses of AI, however, pose a higher risk.

4.5.1 The Core Ethical Challenges

1. Algorithmic Bias in Threat Detection

AI models learn patterns from training data. If that data contains biases, the model will perpetuate them.

Real-World Example:

A security AI trained predominantly on malware targeting Windows systems may:

- Over-detect threats on Windows endpoints (false positives)
- Under-detect threats on Linux/macOS systems (false negatives)
- Allocate disproportionate security resources based on platform, not actual risk

2. Privacy vs. Security Trade-offs

AI security tools often require extensive data collection for effective analysis:

- **User behaviour analytics**: Track all action users take
- **Network monitoring**: Deep packet inspection of traffic
- **Endpoint monitoring**: Process execution, file access, keystrokes
- **Email analysis**: Content scanning for phishing/data exfiltration

3. Explainability and Accountability

Many AI models (especially deep learning) are "black boxes"—they make decisions but can't explain why.

Scenario:

An AI model flags a user account for suspicious activity and automatically disables it. When the user asks why, security analysts can only say "the AI flagged your account as anomalous."

Problems:

- User can't contest the decision (no explanation to challenge)
- Analysts can't verify correctness (no reasoning to audit)

- Legal/HR implications (disabled access may affect job performance)
- Compliance issues

4. Adversarial Use of AI

The same AI techniques used for defense can be weaponized for attack:

Offensive AI Capabilities:

- **AI-generated phishing**: Personalized, contextually accurate phishing emails at scale
- **Deepfake social engineering**: Voice/video impersonation for vishing attacks
- **Automated vulnerability discovery**: AI-powered fuzzing finds 0-days faster
- **Adaptive malware**: Malware that learns to evade detection in real-time
- **AI-powered password cracking**: Neural networks crack complex passwords more efficiently

4.5.2 Key AI Regulation Laws Enterprises Must Track

1. EU AI Act: Global Benchmark

Many people consider the EU AI Act, which was passed in 2024 and went into force in 2025, to be the "gold standard" for AI regulation worldwide. It presents a classification model based on risk:

- **Limited-risk AI**: Requires transparency disclosures (e.g., chatbots must identify themselves as AI).
- **Minimal-risk AI**: Allowed with no restrictions (e.g., spam filters).
- **Unacceptable-risk AI**: Outright banned (e.g., social scoring, manipulative biometric systems).
- **High-risk AI**: Requires conformity assessments, ongoing monitoring, and data governance (e.g., AI in hiring, education, and credit scoring).

The company faces penalties which reach a maximum value of €35 million or 7% of its total yearly global revenue whichever value proves to be greater. General-purpose AI (GPAI) providers face additional transparency obligations regarding training data, model usage, and safety protocols.

2. U.S. State-Led Patchwork

Unlike the EU, the U.S. has no single federal AI law. Instead, states are leading the charge:

- Forty states introduced legislation pertaining to AI in 2024; six states, including California, Colorado, and Connecticut, passed legislation.
- The California Privacy Protection Agency (CPPA) in California was given more authority to enforce laws pertaining to the use of AI in processing consumer data.
- Multiple US states have implemented AI watermarking regulations for generative AI systems to prevent the spread of false information.
- The federal government is currently debating whether to establish a national legal framework that would override existing state legislation. Businesses need to handle multiple compliance requirements which resemble their CCPA and GDPR obligations until the legal debate reaches a resolution.

3. Asia-Pacific Approaches

- **China**: The Cyberspace Administration of China (CAC) announced the launch of a procedure for algorithmic registration and a requirement to disclose all AI-generated media content along with labelling it accordingly.
- **Singapore**: The Model AI Governance Framework serves as a voluntary yet effective guideline which requires organizations to demonstrate their operational processes through transparent and unbiased methods.
- **Japan**: It is interested in the technology and revolution in robotics and artificial intelligence, taking into account the viewpoints about any specific sector.

- **South Korea**: drafting AI legislation with an emphasis on algorithm fairness and data security in consumer applications.
- **Australia**: Teaching AI safety and ethics would pave the way to legislation by 2026.

4. UK's Principles-Based Framework

Rather than adhering to the prescriptive model of the EU, the UK has embraced a principles-based approach instead. The 2025 goals for the UK are:

- Legalizing voluntary agreements on AI safety.
- Creating the AI Safety Institute, which will have the autonomy to audit AI models.
- Giving sector-specific regulators (such as the MHRA for healthcare and the FCA for finance) supervision.

This flexible framework allows innovation while holding businesses accountable.

5. Global Momentum

- According to the Stanford AI Index Report (2025), more than 70 countries currently work on creating or implementing regulations for Artificial Intelligence technologies.
- Global alignment is being pushed by organizations like the G7, UNESCO, and OECD.
- AI governance benchmarks are being formalized by standards organizations like ISO and IEEE.

4.5.3 Legal Challenges and AI in Cyber Law:

1. Privacy Concerns:

- **Data Collection:** The risk of violation of privacy is posed by the large amount of data that is collected by intelligent systems, that occur unless proper management procedures can be implemented. AI applications need to access large data sets because they require this information to operate correctly. The data collection process which includes personal details creates problems regarding consent requirements and data security measures and potential data misuse.

- **Surveillance**: The advanced surveillance systems that use artificial intelligence, which track human activities without their awareness, create problems for both legal systems and ethical standards because they violate people's privacy rights. The implementation of facial recognition systems and behavior analysis tools enables tracking technology to monitor people without their awareness and permission. The technology creates major privacy concerns because governments and corporations have the ability to implement it which could result in a surveillance state.

2. Liability and Accountability:

- **Autonomous Decisions**: When the systems operate without human intervention, the issue of determining the actions of the AI systems becomes challenging. It is also hard to assign the blame of harm done by an AI system that also violates security to either the developer or the operator or the AI system itself since the responsibility may be on both or either. The case poses legal ambiguities of who is responsible of their actions.

- **Regulatory Gaps**: The current legal framework has gaps in the regulation since it lacks specific laws that can be applied in the artificial intelligence technology. This has a problem with the existing legal systems since they have been set in place prior to the popularization of artificial intelligence technologies, and thus, the current legal frameworks cannot be applied by the officials to evaluate cases involving AI. Such a system will generate conflicting results since it will not provide boundaries of interpretation of law when applying regulations.

Ethical governance plus regulatory and technical controls can form the basic framework to develop secure and trustful AI systems that can fulfill the demands of social responsibility.

Multiple Choice Questions (MCQs)

1. **Adversarial machine learning attacks primarily aim to:**
   a. Improve model accuracy
   b. Exploit vulnerabilities in trained AI models
   c. Reduce computational complexity
   d. Enhance data visualization

2. **Which type of adversarial attack manipulates the training data to compromise model behavior?**
   a. Evasion attack
   b. Inference attack
   c. Poisoning attack
   d. Side-channel attack

3. **Model robustness in security-critical AI systems refers to a model's ability to:**
   a. Train faster on large datasets
   b. Resist adversarial inputs and unexpected variations
   c. Use fewer features
   d. Achieve perfect accuracy

4. **Explainable AI (XAI) techniques are especially important in cybersecurity because they:**
   a. Eliminate false positives
   b. Replace security analysts
   c. Improve transparency and trust in model decisions
   d. Increase training data size

5. **Which technique allows multiple organizations to collaboratively train a model without sharing raw data?**
   a. Centralized learning
   b. Transfer learning
   c. Federated Learning (FL)
   d. Supervised learning
6. **Differential Privacy (DP) primarily protects against:**
   a. Malware execution
   b. Model overfitting
   c. Leakage of individual data records
   d. Adversarial examples
7. **Secure multi-party computation enables:**
   a. Faster model inference
   b. Computation on encrypted data without revealing inputs
   c. Centralized data storage
   d. Model compression
8. **AI risk management in cybersecurity focuses on:**
   a. Eliminating all cyber risks
   b. Ignoring low-impact threats
   c. Identifying, assessing, and mitigating AI-related security risks
   d. Replacing compliance frameworks
9. **Regular auditing of AI-based security systems helps organizations to:**
   a. Increase system complexity
   b. Ensure compliance, accountability, and performance consistency
   c. Disable automated decisions
   d. Avoid documentation

10. **Ethical and legal considerations in AI security mainly address:**
    a. Algorithm execution speed
    b. Data center location
    c. Fairness, accountability, transparency, and regulatory compliance
    d. Hardware optimization

Answers

1	2	3	4	5	6	7	8	9	10
b	c	b	c	c	c	b	c	b	c

Chapter 5

Emerging Trends and Future Directions

5.1 Graph-Based Security Analytics and GNN-Powered Defense

Most security tools excel at spotting individual events: an unusual login, a flagged IP, a failed access attempt. Security incidents typically involve multiple activities which spread across different users and systems and environments. The absence of context leads to two problems which include missing essential information and spending unnecessary time pursuing inaccurate results (Sergi et al., 2019).

Security analytics establishes cybersecurity as an intelligence-based field of study. The system uses security data from multiple sources to track user activities between different devices and systems to discover concealed patterns and security threats. The system enables security teams to move from their current state of responding to threats into a more effective approach of detecting and preventing security issues while managing security incidents.

5.1.1 What are Security Analytics?

Security analytics collects security-related data from multiple sources and transforms it into a standardized format which security analysts use to detect and investigate and respond to threats. The system converts unorganized data from network traffic and system logs and identity activity and cloud events into structured information that organizations can use to make decisions.

Security analytics provides monitoring capabilities for multiple users and systems and services through its ability to establish interlinked connectivity. The system detected three security events which included a failed login attempt and an unusual data transfer and the creation of a new administrator account. The three elements appeared to be harmless when examined separately. The assembled evidence indicated that the attackers conducted a synchronized operation.

Modern security analytics platforms use statistical models together with behavior baselining and machine learning or graph analytics to detect anomalies and reveal hidden relationships. The system provides ongoing support at large scale to assist teams in managing high-speed telemetry that comes from their hybrid systems. The security analytics process uses context and correlation data to achieve quicker threat detection and better investigation outcomes and to support informed decision-making.

5.1.2 How Does Security Analytics Work?

Security analytics functions through multiple stages which convert unprocessed telemetry data into usable intelligence. The process improves threat detection accuracy by creating contextual information and eliminating irrelevant data. Teams need to understand these stages because they help in assessing and designing effective analytics workflows (Sergi et al., 2019).

1. Data Collection Across the Attack Surface

The process starts with broad telemetry ingestion from endpoints, network devices, identity systems, cloud services, and applications. The system collects data through four different methods which include agents, log shippers, APIs and SIEM integrations. The attackers can use unprotected areas of security systems to their advantage when organizations lack complete security coverage. The system establishes complete environment visibility through its capacity to collect data in real time from rapidly changing operational settings.

2. Normalization and Enrichment

The security data exists in an unorganized state. The various systems in the network security system produce their logs and telemetry data in different formats which include JSON from cloud providers and syslog from network devices and CSVs from endpoints and the two formats which display different field names and timestamp patterns and lack identification details. The process of data normalization transforms data into a standard structured format which researchers can use for their analytical work.

3. Correlation, Detection, and Threat Modeling

The analytics engine uses its layered detection system to process normalized data which has been enriched with additional content. The system uses rule-based correlation to detect both established attack patterns and unauthorized policy breaches. The system uses behavior baselining to identify security threats by monitoring user and device activity patterns from previous times. The system uses machine learning models to identify small deviations which manual rule systems cannot detect.

Security analytics systems achieve optimal performance through their use of multiple techniques which create an effective detection system that identifies new threats with high accuracy and low false positive rates. The use of graph-based correlation has become a standard practice which enables organizations to connect user activities with device usage across different time periods in order to identify concealed attack pathways.

4. Prioritization and Response Automation

Not every alert deserves the same level of urgency. Security analytics platforms evaluate the context of each event to prioritize what matters most. The system uses asset sensitivity and user privilege level together with behavioral deviation and threat intelligence indicators to calculate risk scores. The system separates critical incidents from low-risk anomalies which can be reviewed at a later time through its ability to detect unusual access to production systems by privileged accounts.

The system uses SOAR integrations to create automated response functions which activate during high-risk incidents. The system requires three specific actions which include account disabling endpoint isolation and network access blocking. Organizations can save investigation time and decrease attacker access time by using automated responses to their known threats.

Investigators access complete case details which include past activities and associated individuals and additional data elements through the investigation queue system that handles less important cases. Security analytics uses risk-based prioritization together with automation to enable security teams to respond to incidents more quickly while handling larger security operations.

5.1.3 Types of Security Analytics

Security analytics uses multiple techniques to detect threats and discover suspicious activities. The different approaches use distinct methods to analyze data because some methods require pattern matching while others need to examine deviations and structural relationships. Modern platforms use multiple techniques to enhance their accuracy while decreasing false positive rates and detecting both established and new types of attacks.

- **Rule-Based Analytics**

  The most traditional detection method uses rules that detect specific conditions which include five failed login attempts within one minute and foreign country login attempts and unauthorized administrator access to sensitive data during non-business hours. The detection system provides clear operation details which users can adjust but it operates as a reactive system. The system detects only known information which results in excessive alert generation that requires precise operational control.

  Rule-based analytics systems remain popular because they help organizations meet their compliance requirements and enforce their access policies and detect known security threats. The system needs additional methods because it cannot identify emerging attack patterns which remain unknown to its current capabilities.

- **Behavioral Baseline Analytics**

  The method creates user device and service behavior models which it uses to identify uncommon patterns instead of establishing known patterns as its starting point. The system creates a baseline which enables it to detect any subsequent deviations from established performance standards. The system will identify a user who logs in at strange times and transfers high volumes of data while accessing uncommon resources.

  This method is especially successful at identifying insider threats and credential compromises and lateral movement attacks because it detects behavioral changes that do not match established patterns. The system establishes baseline measurements through actual user behavior instead of using permanent programming rules which results in enhanced adaptability to different operational environments.

- **Machine Learning-Based Analytics**

  Machine learning is a combination of statistical modeling and pattern recognition techniques to improve the security analytics capability. The ML system is able to identify complex relationships between data points and identify small deviations in large high-dimensional data sets.

  As an example, an anomaly detector algorithm could raise an alarm on a mix of user position, device model, and access time that has never been known in the history. The clustering models employ frequent patterns of behavior to determine the users who exhibit abnormal behavior. Some systems use supervised learning to differentiate between harmless and harmful activities by using training data that has been properly labeled.

  Machine learning detects common patterns in data which enables it to identify significant atypical events. The system requires precise adjustments because of its critical need to prove operational functions in security settings which demand understanding the reasons behind alerts.

- **Graph-Based Analytics**

  The field of graph analytics examines the structural relationships between different entities. The system tracks entity interactions throughout time instead of processing events as separate occurrences. An attacker starts with a low-privilege account to access a second machine which allows him to gain higher privileges before he enters a protected database. The assessment of attack steps through individual alerts shows no detection. The assessment shows that all steps form an attack path which becomes evident through analysis of their connection in a graph.

  The detection of multi-stage threats together with privilege escalation and lateral movement and policy misconfigurations benefits from graph-based methods. Security environments need to be represented through graph-based methods because both their relationships and their events have equal importance in their security assessment. Security analytics platforms need to use multiple techniques instead of depending on a single method for their security operations. The system uses multiple techniques which include speed and clarity rules together with performance baselines and machine learning pattern recognition and graph analytics to establish context and reachability. The system uses a two-level alerting system which provides high-confidence alerts and advanced investigation capabilities.

5.1.4 Graph-Powered Security Analytics with Puppy Graph

The process of threat detection requires more than simple anomaly detection because it requires knowledge of how various incidents connect with each other. The activities of lateral movement and privilege escalation together with indirect access methods extend across various users and multiple systems throughout different periods. The complete picture remains hidden from traditional tools because they cannot detect these relationships.

Puppy Graph provides a solution for this problem by making relationship-based detection more accessible to users. Puppy Graph provides a real-time graph query engine which operates without needing any extraction, transformation, or loading processes to enable users to model and examine their interconnected data from their current SQL systems. Puppy Graph establishes a direct link to relational data sources which enables users to access their data as graph structures without needing to create an independent pipeline for graph database access. With Puppy Graph, you create a graph schema that shows how users, sessions, and resources connect with one another. Can then query those relationships using familiar graph languages like openCypher or Gremlin.

Analyzing the security using this approach has the advantage of the following:

- **Real-time, multi-hop investigation:** Puppy Graph provides quick access to recursive queries which enable users to track user activities from their initial session to their final resource usage. This capability helps security teams discover concealed lateral movement activities together with their associated access path.
- **Flexible graph modeling:** The system enables users to create different graph views which display the same data, thus enabling teams to concentrate on their specific needs through two different access paths which show identity relationships and API access paths and infrastructure dependencies.
- **No data duplication:** There is no additional requirement of storage since the existing data itself is directly queried. The system achieves reduced complexity and lower operating costs through this design.
- **Built-in visualization:** Puppy Graph includes a native interface for querying and exploring graphs visually, so analysts can investigate threats and relationships without building custom dashboards or exporting data.

Why Graph Analytics?

The direction and strength of links between items in a graph may be identified using graph analytics. Relationships between two items at a moment as well as the overall structural features of the graph are highlighted. Road networks, communications networks, social networks, online pages and linkages, and financial transaction data are a few types of data that function well with graphs. Graph analytics has proven especially helpful in doing the following:

- Identify financial offenses like money laundering
- Recognize fraudulent behaviors and transactions
- Analyze influencers within social media groups.
- Analyze recommendations based on consumer ratings or purchases.
- Determine the vulnerabilities in the transportation, water, and electricity networks.
- Improve airline, retail, and manufacturing routes.

Top Graph Analytics Use Cases

Create systems that provide recommendations. Businesses may create sophisticated recommendation engines that react to consumers' online activity in real time by determining the connections and frequencies between customers, social media, and product data.

Identify fraud. You can model data relationships at scale with great flexibility using graph analytics, which enables you to quickly analyze massive volumes of transactional data to spot fraud in real time.

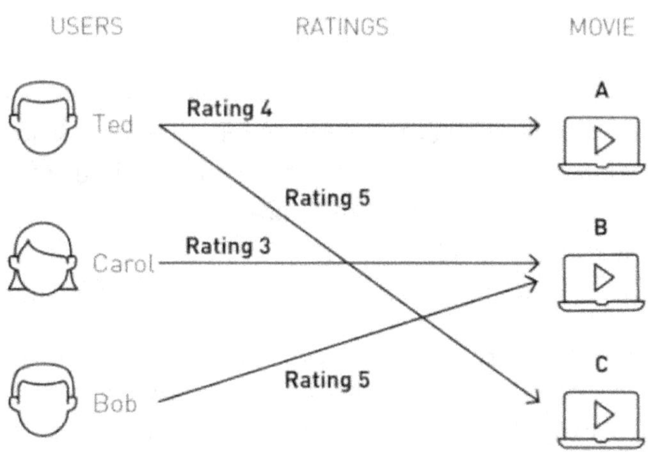

Figure 5.1: Build recommendation systems

Source: (Nvidia, 2025)

Respect legal requirements. Businesses in a variety of industries must comply with laws including GDPR, PCI/DSS, and HIPAA. These requirements mandate that you have insight into the data as it travels through several corporate systems whenever you gather personal information about clients. Graph analytics provides a visual depiction of the data moving through various systems, making it much simpler to trace sensitive data via business systems. This makes it easier for you to comply with regulations.

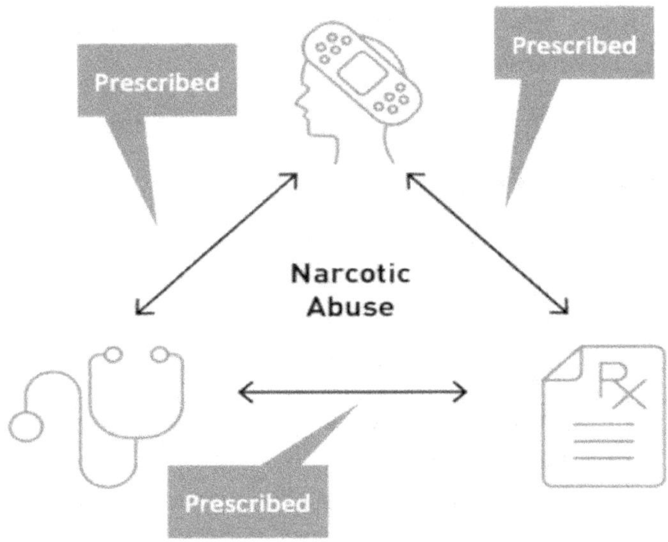

Figure 5.2: Detect Fraud

Source: (Nvidia, 2025)

IAM stands for master identity and access management. It's difficult to decide who should have access to sensitive data and apps, both on-premises and in the cloud. A more reliable, cross-platform, real-time administration of all required data to identify relationships and expedite safe and secure IAM is made possible by graph analytics.

Learn about the effectiveness of the supply chain. Globalization has made company supply chains more intricate than before. You may model these intricate linkages and gain much more transparency into any supply chain operational inefficiencies by using graph analytics.

5.1.5 Graph Neural Network (GNN)

Graph neural networks, or GNNs for short, are machine learning software systems that analyze graph-based data. The nodes and edges of the input graphs are the two main components that GNNs employ to draw conclusions through deep learning.

The input data points are represented by the nodes, or vertices on the graph, and the connections between the data points are represented by the edges, or lines connecting the nodes.

Graph neural networks can understand data supplied to them as a graph by examining nodes and edges. They may then use this interpretation to solve problems and make predictions.

Online platforms and several industry sectors can benefit from such decision-making. For instance, GNNs may identify abnormalities in those data sets as well as make predictions by identifying patterns between edges and nodes that, for example, reflect relationships between seemingly unrelated addresses. This aids in identifying critical outliers in datasets or suspect internet activities.

One type of data structure is a graph neural network, which is a particular method for handling, storing, and analyzing data. GNNs are distinct data structures because they represent a particular interpretation of the term "graph."

The computer science-specific context of GNNs refers to a graph that is a representation of the data in a certain data structure, made up of nodes and edges, as opposed to a standard graph with an x-axis and y-axis.

5.1.6 How Powerful Are Graph Neural Networks?

Because they efficiently do representation learning and create correct models of the data they receive, graph neural networks are extremely potent tools. The process by which a software system automatically finds patterns in the data it receives is known as representation learning.

Because of its special ability to identify many data connections and/or abnormalities, GNNs are able to perform representation learning; the node-and-vertex organization yields unique insights. They thereby influence people's capacity to solve problems and make decisions in the actual world.

The fact that graph neural networks (GNNs) are mostly (but not entirely) self-sufficient—that is, they can identify their points of input without as much human aid as other machine learning systems would need—makes GNNs particularly potent.

5.1.7 Five Applications of Graph Neural Networks

This includes five graph neural network applications. And these are only five important instances of applications that might go on forever.

Graph neural networks may be able to examine a trail of data that includes users, their transactions, and their accounts.

1. Fraud Prevention

GNN analysis can identify new accounts that might be linked to a history of harmful conduct, thereby designating those accounts as "guilty by association." It is possible to identify potentially suspicious people using specific features of a device or browser fingerprint. Is it possible that two seemingly unrelated individuals are shipping to the same location while having identical browser settings? This could be sufficient to close the triangle in a significant and practical manner.

GNNs can thus be utilized to forecast future actions that the malevolent entity could do. We'll talk about this system later. It's called link analysis.

2. Online Safety

Graph neural networks are essential for improving online safety in social media, as was previously discussed.

GNNs' ability to apply graph theory to online networks makes it possible for people to comprehend important aspects of users' online behavior. Social media analysis is the name given to this method of cybersecurity.

3. Medicine

Graph neural networks are able to examine patient data, including age and gender, and identify patterns related to those variables.

This enables medical practitioners to spot patterns in their diagnoses and therapies that are unique to different patient populations.

4. Computer Vision

Computer vision is an artificial intelligence system that enables computers to scan pictures, classify them, and draw inferences from the categorization.

By recognizing patterns and abnormalities in different pictures and drawing inferences from them, GNNs can improve the capabilities of computer vision systems.

The essential area of cancer screening requires X-rays to identify abnormal tissue patterns which doctors use to assess patients during their cancer screening procedures.

5. Geolocation

GNN technology improves the geolocation of navigation systems like Google Maps to ensure that the drivers are given the true estimated time of arrival information. Graph neural networks are able to provide the right estimation of journey time due to their capacity to handle numerous nodes that incorporate traffic conditions and speed limits and weather patterns.

5.2 AI for Cyber-Physical Systems and Critical Infrastructure

The study establishes that artificial intelligence in Cyber-Physical Systems (CPS) invents new technological remedies that enhance operational performance on various kinds of applications. The article explores the correlation between these two areas and exposes their existing challenges and how they will evolve in the future to self-driving automobiles and tailor-made learning.

5.2.1 The Role of Artificial Intelligence in Cyber-Physical Systems

Artificial intelligence serves as an engine for improving the operation of cyber-physical systems, which offers the capacity of the systems to learn and change their behaviors as they make decisions using the available information. These machine learning algorithms that fall under the artificial intelligence discipline allow organizations to examine complex data trends and carry out predictive modeling activities. The system proves to be worth in cases that demand smart resolutions to handle virtual and physical components that demand flexibility.

- **Predictive Maintenance in Manufacturing:**

  The manufacturing industry relies on predictive maintenance that is run with the help of AI technology that acts as a part of cyber-physical systems. The conventional maintenance system demands that the maintenance jobs should be carried out at certain times that poses two issues. This system is based on AI algorithms, which will help to predict the upcoming equipment failures by tracking real-time sensor data of machinery equipment. The system is predictive to facilitate the maintenance work that reduces the amount of time spent on operations, but rather produces more work at a high efficiency.

- **Smart Grids for Energy Management:**

  AI technology applied in conjunction with CPS systems develops an advanced power grid system that promotes more efficient energy delivery. Smart grids apply AI algorithms to analyze the data streams that their sensors and smart meters generate, which are in large quantities.

  The analysis allows making the accurate predictions of the energy usage patterns which contribute to the improved distribution techniques and the higher grid system reliability. The system has an increased efficiency because of its sustainable energy management activities.

- **Healthcare Revolution: AI in Cyber-Physical Medical Systems:**

  Medical data collection and the data analysis processes and patient outcome improvement activities within the health sector have been revolutionized through artificial intelligence. Cyber-Physical Medical Systems (CPMS) are AI algorithms that apply to bridge the linkage between wearable technology, medical devices, and electronic health record systems.

  The system enables health workers to access patients at any given time and observe the health conditions and develop personalized treatment strategies. The integration of AI technology with Cyber-Physical Systems in the healthcare sector allows physicians to obtain higher diagnostic outcomes as well as enhance the process of patient care.

5.2.2 Challenges and Considerations

Using artificial intelligence to apply to cyber-physical systems yields several benefits to its users but poses a number of challenges. The three major security concerns which need particular attention are the violation of data privacy and threats of system vulnerability. The creation of AI algorithms means that organizations will have to employ robust cybersecurity systems that withstand the types of threats that arise to ensure that their CPS systems are not compromised.

- **Security Concerns and Countermeasures:**

  Cyber systems have cybersecurity threats since the elements of the cybersystem are networked. The creation of more sophisticated AI algorithms results in a greater capacity of hackers to follow their attack plans. The security of cyber-physical systems brings a necessity to organizations to consider powerful encryption mechanisms and authentication protocols in conjunction with the continuous monitoring of the security system. Integrity maintenance of systems needs to be implemented with regular updates and vulnerability patches.

- **Ethical Considerations in AI Integration:**

  Applications of AI in CPS systems have shown that they present ethical challenges that impact upon three research fields such as protection of privacy and accountability practices and decision-making processes. The increasing autonomy of these systems poses important questions about who is responsible for all that they do, along with their impacts on both individual persons and society in general. The creation of ethical standards along with regulatory environments and open-minded decision-making processes serves as a crucial condition to overcome ethical problems emerging because of the introduction of AI to CPS systems.

5.2.3 Future Perspectives: Advancements and Innovations

The news of AI integration into the Cyber-Physical Systems is a dynamic field of research that has significant potential of growth in technology. The increasing performance of AI algorithms, along with the development of computing power, will allow CPS systems to attain new performance possibilities that will open new opportunities in technological advancement. Of interest are some of the following areas:

1. Edge Computing and AI in CPS

By embedding AI in ubiquitous computing, the management of data would then become conditional upon the immediate manipulation of data at the source. The system achieves three main benefits through its design which decreases waiting times while improving the capacity for immediate decision-making and reducing the load on its main cloud computing systems. The combination of edge computing with artificial intelligence enables new opportunities for development in self-driving cars and intelligent urban environments and automated industrial systems.

2. Swarm Intelligence and CPS

Swarm intelligence develops from social organisms that exhibit collective behavior, which scientists now study for application in cyber-physical systems. The combination of swarm intelligence and artificial intelligence creates systems that display emergent behavior through the teamwork of multiple basic units that work together to solve intricate challenges. This method improves CPS systems through better adaptability, increased system capacity, and stronger protection across multiple applications, including traffic control, emergency response, and environmental assessment.

3. Robotics and Industry 4.0

The manufacturing sector requires AI and CPS technology to develop its Industry 4.0 framework. The smart factories now use AI-powered robots as their essential operating components. The AI-powered robots work together with human operators to achieve production goals and boost total productivity.

The robots use machine learning algorithms to adjust their behavior based on new environment conditions, which makes them suitable for operation in changing manufacturing settings. The future of manufacturing, which includes Industry 4.0 development, will depend on AI-based cyber-physical systems as essential technology.

4. Environmental Monitoring and AI

The current implementation of artificial intelligence solutions within cyber-physical systems allows for environmental monitoring, which directly supports efforts to combat climate change, pollution, and natural disaster challenges. Smart sensors equipped with AI algorithms monitor air quality, water levels, seismic activities, and additional environmental parameters in real time. The initial environmental risk detection system needs this information because it enables immediate response activities. Organizations can use AI technology in CPS systems to collect environmental data, which they use to research complex environmental patterns that enable sustainable resource management and disaster preparedness solutions.

5. Human-Machine Collaboration and Augmented Reality

Human-machine relationships in cyber-physical systems develop new forms of collaboration because artificial intelligence systems become integrated into these systems. Augmented Reality (AR) applications, which use artificial intelligence technology, enable workers to project digital content onto real-world environments, thus enhancing their operational accuracy.

Technicians in the maintenance field demonstrate human-machine collaboration through their use of augmented reality systems, which provide them with real-time information and guidance to enhance their work performance and decrease their error rates.

6. Personalized Learning and AI in Education

The educational system in CPS uses AI technology to create new learning experiences for students. Personalized learning platforms use AI algorithms to study individual learning styles and preferences, and the learning progress of students. The educational content and activities are customized based on this information to create an optimal learning experience for every student. The implementation of AI technology in CPS creates a flexible learning environment which helps students engage better with their studies and remember information for longer periods.

5.2.4 Cyber Security in Critical Infrastructure Best Practices

Best practices of cyber security in critical infrastructure, which include:

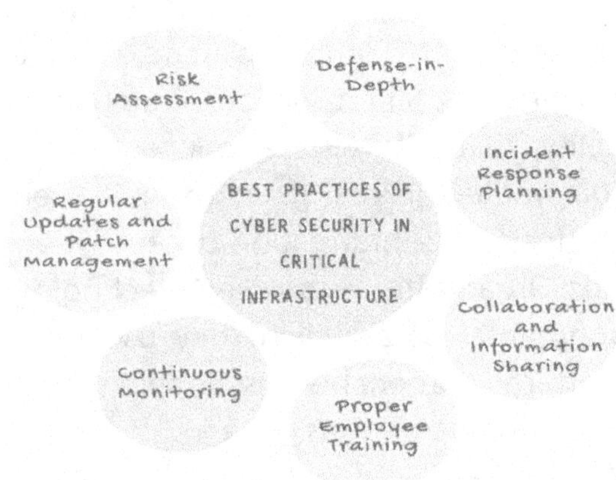

Figure 5.3: Cyber Security Best Practices in Critical Infrastructure

Source: (Geeksforgeeks, 2026)

1. **Risk Assessment**
    - Identifies threats and vulnerabilities
    - Helps prioritize security investments
    - Forms the foundation of security planning
2. **Defense-in-Depth**
    - Uses multiple layers of security
    - Includes firewalls, IDS, encryption, and access control
    - Reduces impact of single security failure
3. **Incident Response Planning**
    - Predefined procedures for cyber incidents
    - Ensures quick detection, containment, and recovery
    - Minimizes operational disruption
4. **Collaboration and Information Sharing**
    - Encourages cooperation between governments and organizations
    - Improves threat intelligence and preparedness
5. **Employee Training**
    - Educates staff about phishing and social engineering
    - Reduces human-related security risks
6. **Continuous Monitoring**
    - Real-time detection of suspicious activity
    - Enables proactive defense mechanisms
7. **Patch Management**
    - Regular updates close known vulnerabilities
    - Reduces chances of exploitation

5.2.5 Examples of Cyber Security in Critical Infrastructure

Here are some examples of cybersecurity in critical infrastructure:

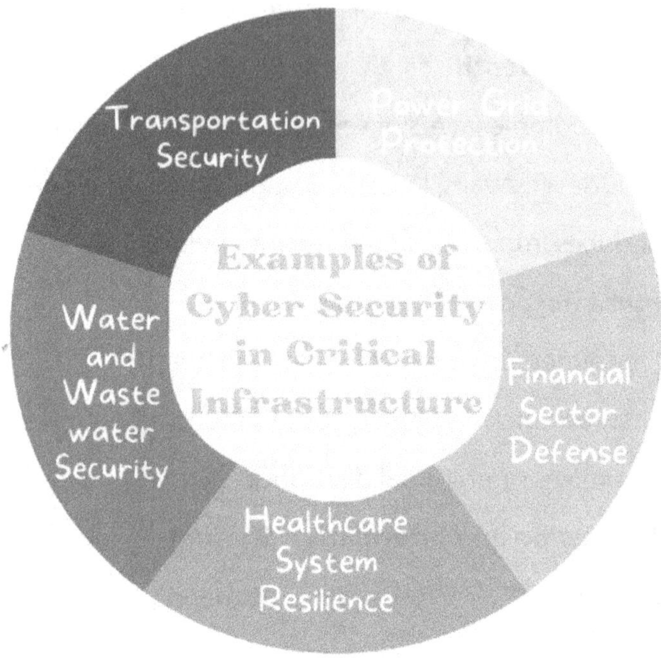

Figure 5.4: Examples of Cyber Security in Critical Infrastructure

Source: (Geeksforgeeks, 2026)

1. **Transportation Security**
   - Encryption of communication networks
   - Biometric authentication at airports and ports
   - Restricted access to critical assets
2. **Power Grid Protection**
   - Firewalls and intrusion detection systems
   - Network traffic monitoring and anomaly detection
   - Regular penetration testing and vulnerability assessments

3. **Financial Sector Defense**
    - Protection of banking and payment systems
    - Fraud detection and anomaly monitoring
    - Use of multi-factor authentication and tokenization
4. **Healthcare System Resilience**
    - Protection of electronic health records (EHRs)
    - Securing medical devices and telemedicine platforms
    - Use of encryption and secure authentication
    - Emergency response planning to ensure patient care continuity
5. **Water and Wastewater Security**
    - Segregation of operational networks
    - Protection of Industrial Control Systems (ICS)
    - Firmware integrity checks and access control
    - Cybersecurity drills and training exercises

5.3 AI-Enabled Autonomous Cyber Defense Systems

AI systems use advanced algorithms together with machine learning methods to improve their ability to detect cyber threats and to develop strategies for handling these threats. The cybersecurity systems that use AI technology process extensive data sets to detect existing security threats while enabling security personnel to make quick and informed choices. The system enables security teams to automate their basic activities through its ability to conduct vulnerability assessments and analyze system logs and perform system checks.

AI in cybersecurity improves threat detection methods while it streamlines the process of managing vulnerabilities and it automates response times to security incidents. The system enhances cybersecurity operations through its ability to identify phishing threats and its capacity to analyze user activities and its function that permits organizations to safeguard their confidential information.

5.3.1 The Evolution of Cyber Defense

Cybersecurity threats today extend beyond traditional viruses and phishing attacks. The present security environment includes three main threats which are artificial intelligence-based cybercrime, state-sponsored cyber-attacks and specialized ransomware attacks that exploit all digital weaknesses in cloud systems and supply chain operations. The current security environment requires organizations to adopt advanced security systems because conventional rule-based security systems have become ineffective against modern advanced persistent threats.

The new solution from Nano Matrix Secure introduces a new security approach which uses artificial intelligence to identify threats while safeguarding data through machine learning and behavioral analytics and digital forensics methods which create real-time threat detection and response systems. The implementation of artificial intelligence has become essential for CIOs and CISOs and business executives because it enables organizations to maintain ongoing protection against cyber threats in today's highly connected environment.

5.3.2 The Case for AI in Modern Cybersecurity

AI transforms how enterprises identify and mitigate risks. AI-driven security systems use global threat intelligence and network behavior and contextual anomalies to operate because they learn continuously from these data sources instead of using manual monitoring or static signatures as their primary detection method.

- Real-time detection of zero-day exploits and polymorphic malware
- Predictive analytics that forecast emerging attack patterns

- Automated response mechanisms that contain and neutralize threats instantly

According to Gartner, by 2026, over 60% of Security Operations Centers (SOCs) will integrate AI analytics as a primary tool for continuous threat detection and risk scoring.

5.3.3 How AI-Powered Threat Detection Works

AI-driven cybersecurity operates through several interlinked layers:

1. Data Aggregation & Normalization

AI systems gather data from firewalls and endpoints and IoT devices and cloud systems to create standardized information which establishes a behavioral baseline that enables them to identify minor deviations from normal behavior.

2. Machine Learning Algorithms

Nano Matrix AI uses supervised learning and unsupervised learning to discover patterns that show abnormal behavior which helps the system detect new security threats before they become serious.

3. Behavioral Analytics

The AI system improves its models by studying human and machine activities while it detects unauthorized access attempts and privilege upgrades and suspicious data movement.

4. Automated Response & Forensics

The AI-based threat detection system of Nano Matrix uses automated response procedures to identify and separate infected devices while it automatically removes access rights from unauthorized users.

5.3.4 Key Benefits of AI-Powered Cyber Defense

1. Faster Threat Identification

The AI is set to pick up on the unusual activity in the matter of milliseconds causing proactive defense to occur before the hacking even takes place.

2. Reduced False Positives

Adaptive learning, in lowering the number of false alarms, hence allows cybersecurity teams to focus on critical incidents.

3. Continuous Evolution

AI learns dynamically unlike static tools, thereby evolving with every new threat vector and dataset.

4. Compliance-Ready by Design

Nano Matrix AI achieves full compliance with ISO 27001 and NIST 800-53 and GDPR and APRA CPS 234 requirements because it provides documentation for the auditing process and maintains records of its response actions.

5.4 Edge AI, Federated Learning, and Distributed Defense Models

Edge AI technology processes the data through AI at the network edge directly on the devices which results in real-time decision-making, reduced latency, and improved privacy. Federated Learning is a technique where a number of devices are able to train a common global model together without the need to share raw data which means that the data security is protected while the collective intelligence is increased. The technologies together give support to distributed defense models, which work on the principle that edge devices will first detect and then mitigate the threats locally while simultaneously being a part of a global security framework that is coordinated thus increasing the resilience, adaptability, and privacy in cyber defense.

5.4.1 Understanding Edge AI and Why It Matters for Security

Instead of depending on centralized cloud infrastructure, edge AI refers to the application of machine learning models directly on edge devices or local networks. It also describes the use of edge data to power a closed-loop, two-way system: Read → Examine → Automate (back).

Security sector does have a lot more to offer for the initiative.

- **Low Latency**: The edge processes data at its location or through its closest edge node, which enables instant decision-making that supports critical applications such as real-time surveillance and intrusion detection and law enforcement.
- **Privacy and Security**: The edge AI system protects confidential data through its ability to process information locally because this function reduces cyber threats and provides better protection for hidden data. The system requires all its distributed components to undergo monitoring and patching operations in order to maintain proper cybersecurity practices.
- **Bandwidth Optimization**: The process of sending substantial security videos together with sensor information to the cloud for analysis leads to both increased expenses and decreased operational efficiency. Edge AI decreases bandwidth costs because it processes essential data on-site while sending only required notifications to security staff.
- **Resilience and Reliability**: Edge AI provides uninterrupted operation capability which works effectively in locations that either lack Internet access or have restricted Internet access. This technology works best for remote security monitoring and smart surveillance systems and mission-critical applications.

The combination of low-latency connections with next-generation networks and improved AI models enables businesses to implement intelligence systems at their data creation sites which results in new security and public safety innovations.

5.4.2 Understanding Federated Learning

The research foundation of federated learning extends to its primary element which consists of deep learning neural networks. Each edge node operates as a client because it stores its data on-site to develop its own training model.

Different amounts of data can be used to train each local model. The amount of samples received from each model is taken into account by the server while updating the global model. Additionally, the server does not wait for an instant response after requesting that an edge node take part in updating the global model since the connection from the edge nodes to the server is asynchronous. In terms of efficiency, this is really desired.

It should be noted that the edge nodes preserve confidentiality by limiting access to their local data and refraining from sharing it with other nodes. The central FL server receives the local model weights and combines them into a single global model.

The global model may be updated by the server via a variety of techniques. When the model is finished, all participating edge nodes receive it from the server. Without ever seeing their data, every edge node now possesses all the insights gathered from every other edge node.

While the majority of AI and ML applications are employed by businesses to obtain a competitive edge, there are other situations in which businesses have an incentive to collaborate; cybersecurity is a good example. In this instance, the objective is to prevent the hackers from entering their internal networks and infecting their computer systems in order to counter a common danger.

Cybersecurity Mesh Architecture: A Distributed Defense Model

Cybersecurity Mesh Architecture is a decentralized security approach that treats security as a network of interconnected security controls, rather than a single, centralized perimeter. Imagine a mesh network, where each node (device, application, user) has its own security policies and controls, communicating and cooperating with other nodes to maintain overall security. This security approach differs from existing security systems which require only one firewall or security information and event management (SIEM) system to protect their entire network.

The CMA system shows its full value because it can adapt to new situations while maintaining its operational strength. The network security system protects most of its components because each node has its own security measures that operate independently from other nodes. The system's distributed architecture creates major challenges for attackers who try to obtain complete control of the system. The primary element that enables CMA to function depends on "micro-segmentation" which creates network partitions that restrict breach damage across the system.

Key Components

Several pillars on which the efficacy of the Cybersecurity Mesh Architecture lies are:

- **Micro-segmentation**: The network needs to be divided into smaller sections which operate independently to control the effects of a security breach. Virtual LANs (VLANs) and network segmentation tools plus additional technologies enable this goal to be reached.
- **Zero Trust Security**: The security model operates without trust assumptions because it requires verification of all users and devices before granting access to resources which can be accessed from any location.
- **Security Service Mesh (SSM):** A dedicated infrastructure layer that provides security services to microservices and applications. Usually this system implements technologies such as Istio and Linkerd, etc.
- **Data Loss Prevention (DLP):** Different approaches are used by the organization to prevent unauthorized leaks of data with a security value.
- **Security Information and Event Management (SIEM):** Security log collection system operates by examining various data sources to detect and address possible security threats. The SIEM system within a CMA environment enables the organization to connect distributed network events through its event correlation capabilities.
- **Cloud Access Security Broker (CASB):** «It serves as a security policy enforcement point for cloud-based applications and services.»

Core Benefits

The core benefits of adopting a CMA include:

- **Enhanced Security Posture**: To successfully traverse the system, Trojans must combat the distributed nature of systems.
- **Improved Resilience**: The architecture distributes, and any break-in damage get isolated, meaning the part cannot affect the other if active hacking did spoil something inside the shell of this structure.
- **Better Adaptability**: The CMA can be highly flexible to changes in the networking environment, making the system well-suited to the early integration of new devices or applications.
- **Reduced Complexity**: CMA appears difficult to understand but it helps organizations manage their security operations through its automated functions and detailed security monitoring capabilities.
- **Improved Visibility**: The CMA tool provides better visibility over the security posture for the whole of the network.

5.5 Future Research Directions and Evolving Cyber Threats

Our cybersecurity analysts continuously research to investigate emerging threats which they use to develop new defense strategies against attacks. We have identified several important cybersecurity trends which we have observed during recent times and which we expect to persist in the future.

5.5.1 APTs expanding their tricks

Advanced persistent threats (APTs) are highly sophisticated, well-funded groups that often receive state sponsorship to conduct their operations against particular organizations or entire industry sectors with the goal of intelligence gathering and operational disruption.

The APTs began using their proximity-based and infrastructure-targeted attacks more frequently during 2024. For instance, APT 28 used the "nearest neighbor attack" to penetrate Wi-Fi networks by attacking devices that were close to their primary targets. The attackers used physical proximity to defeat some security systems because they focused on exploiting an environmental weakness.

Organizations should consider non-digital attack vectors and implement zero-trust architectures that extend to physical environments. The approach will prove especially important for energy and finance and government sectors.

5.5.2 Attacks that circumvent MFA protections

Field Effect released their findings about a new adversary-in-the-middle attack in 2024 which enabled threats to intercept all communications between two parties while they performed their attack to obtain passwords and session tokens. The attackers used this method to obtain unauthorized access to accounts after they successfully intercepted credentials needed for multi-factor authentication.

Our investigation uncovered a campaign which attackers used Axios-based lookalike M365 login pages to steal credentials from victims. The fraudulent pages directed victims to authenticate themselves through proxy authentication requests which collected their passwords and MFA codes. The attackers utilized the Axios HTTP client to access M365 accounts while successfully evading MFA requirements.

The Mamba MFA Phishing Kit functioned as a phishing-as-a-service platform which enabled cybercriminals to conduct AiTM attacks with greater efficiency. For a small subscription fee, threat actors could capture authentication tokens, circumvent MFA, and compromise M365 accounts.

5.5.3 Evolving Cyber Threats & Hacking Techniques

While there are various hacking methods that threat actors use to accomplish their objectives, the most common attack methods consist of malware and phishing and ransomware attacks. The article presents different hacking techniques which will be explored throughout the text.

- **Malware, Phishing, and Ransomware Attacks**

  The most prevalent types of cybercrime which people commit involve three types of attacks. which unethical black hat hackers use to commit their illicit activities. Malware describes all software threats which hackers use to break into computer systems while phishing describes all fraudulent attempts to obtain private information through unauthorized identity deception. Phishing attacks usually occur when attackers send emails that appear to come from a company which requests users to enter their login credentials or share their confidential details.

  Ransomware attacks currently represent one of the most rapidly expanding threats which cybersecurity experts need to address. After attackers gain unauthorized access to vital data or systems, they can lock the information until the victim pays a ransom for its release. The method proves especially harmful when used against essential systems which support hospitals and energy facilities.

- **SQL Injection and Cross-Site Scripting (XSS)**

  SQL injection attacks rank among the most frequent methods of attacking websites. Hackers exploit security weaknesses which exist in online forms that request users to provide information like their username and date of birth. Instead of entering this information, bad actors are able to "inject" lines of code that the system will unknowingly execute. This can result in access to secure information asked for by the form or even access to the underlying servers themselves. Cross-site scripting (XSS) attacks are also web-based. However, these programs are executed on the user side when they click on a malicious link that often brings them to a legitimate website while also stealing sensitive information, such as cookies, from the user's device.

- **Social Engineering and Pretexting**

  Social engineering and pretexting rely on the attacker's ability to create and exploit a relationship with their victim. Pretexting refers to the initial contact stages where the hacker develops some fraudulent pretext such as having met the target at a conference or being an old school acquaintance. This phase typically lasts only as long as it is necessary for the attacker to feel that they have laid a significant enough foundation to bypass some of their target's better instincts. At this point, attackers will often attempt to get their target to divulge sensitive information or even do something as simple as click on a malicious link or attachment that they would typically avoid from an unknown sender.

- **Exploiting Vulnerabilities and Using Zero-Day Attacks**

  Unlike the previously mentioned attacks, exploiting vulnerabilities and launching zero day attacks do not require any level of involvement on the part of the victim. These approaches focus on fundamental flaws in a program or system that can exist in software or hardware. Once attackers recognize these targets, they deploy malware that takes advantage of these specific weaknesses. While some vulnerabilities are known to developers and patches are developed, zero-day attacks are completely unforeseen flaws without currently existing solutions.

- **Distributed Denial-of-Service (DDoS)**

  A distributed denial-of-service (DDoS) is a type of hacking attack that looks to overwhelm a server or network with a flood of information requests. Attackers typically will employ a system of connected devices that they have infected with malware that allows them to be controlled remotely. Hackers use these devices, known as bots, in an orchestrated attack that disrupts service and prevents legitimate traffic from accessing a site. Most recently, an example of this kind of attack can be found in the Microsoft Azure outage that disrupted Azure services for over eight hours.

- **Cybersecurity Prevention Measures**

  When it comes to defending against attackers and their various types of hacking, there is no one-size-fits-all approach. However, there are some agreed upon best practices that should be maintained industry wide. Every organization should implement robust firewalls and intrusion detection systems. Effective firewalls are the first layer of defense that dictate what enters and exits a controlled network and prevents most threats from even reaching their intended targets. Intrusion detection systems allow for swift mitigation when penetration occurs, minimizing lateral movement and compartmentalizing damage.

  It is also necessary for every organization to regularly test its own defenses by conducting regular security audits and performing penetration testing on its systems. Security audits can be employed to evaluate a number of aspects of an organization's security in areas such as vulnerabilities or compliance. Penetration testing is a specific type of security audit in which an auditor simulates an attack and tries to gain control of the system. This can be particularly valuable in identifying unforeseen weaknesses.

Multiple Choice Questions (MCQs)

1. **Graph-based security analytics primarily model cybersecurity data as:**
   a. Independent numerical records
   b. Sequential time-series signals
   c. Nodes and edges representing entities and relationships
   d. Image-like feature maps

2. **Graph Neural Networks (GNNs) are especially effective in cybersecurity because they:**
   a. Eliminate the need for labeled data
   b. Capture relational and structural patterns in attack graphs
   c. Require minimal computational resources
   d. Replace traditional encryption methods
3. **AI applications in cyber-physical systems (CPS) focus mainly on securing:**
   a. Virtual machines only
   b. Physical processes integrated with computational and communication components
   c. Standalone desktop systems
   d. Offline databases
4. **Which characteristic makes securing critical infrastructure particularly challenging for AI-based systems?**
   a. Lack of real-time data
   b. High tolerance for system downtime
   c. Safety-critical operations and real-time constraints
   d. Complete isolation from networks
5. **AI-enabled autonomous cyber defense systems are designed to:**
   a. Operate only under human supervision
   b. Perform reactive defense after attacks
   c. Detect, decide, and respond to threats with minimal human intervention
   d. Replace legal and governance frameworks

6. **A key risk associated with fully autonomous cyber defense systems is:**
    a. Reduced automation
    b. Over-reliance on static rules
    c. Unintended actions due to incorrect model decisions
    d. Increased hardware lifespan
7. **Edge AI in cybersecurity is primarily motivated by the need for:**
    a. Centralized data processing
    b. High-latency communication
    c. Real-time, low-latency threat detection close to data sources
    d. Manual security monitoring
8. **Federated learning supports distributed defense models by:**
    a. Sharing raw security logs across nodes
    b. Centralizing sensitive datasets
    c. Training models collaboratively without exchanging local data
    d. Eliminating privacy concerns completely
9. **One major future research direction in AI-driven cybersecurity is:**
    a. Dependence on static signatures
    b. Ignoring adversarial threats
    c. Developing resilient AI models against evolving attack strategies
    d. Reducing dataset diversity

10. **Evolving cyber threats in the AI era are best characterized by:**
    a. Predictable and slow-changing patterns
    b. Manual exploitation techniques only
    c. Adaptive, intelligent, and AI-powered attack behaviors
    d. Complete elimination of human attackers

Answers

1	2	3	4	5	6	7	8	9	10
c	b	b	c	c	c	c	c	c	c

Bibliography

Agarwal, P. (2024). Spotting Rare Events: Anomaly Detection Techniques with Machine Learning. *Medium*. https://medium.com/@agarwal_pulkit/spotting-rare-events-anomaly-detection-techniques-with-machine-learning-6e36faff71e9

Fortinet. (2025). *Ransomware: Types, Examples & Removal Tactics*. https://www.fortinet.com/resources/cyberglossary/ransomware

Geeksforgeeks. (2025). *Privacy-Preserving in Machine Learning*. https://www.geeksforgeeks.org/machine-learning/privacy-preserving-in-machine-learning/

Geeksforgeeks. (2026). *Understanding Cyber Security in Critical Infrastructure*. https://www.geeksforgeeks.org/computer-networks/understanding-cyber-security-in-critical-infrastructure/

Gill, N. S. (2024). Deep Learning in Cybersecurity: Threat Detection and Defense. *Xenonstack-Logo*. https://www.xenonstack.com/blog/deep-learning-in-cybersecurity

Harris, D. (2023). *Virtual Reality Visualisations for Cyber Security*. https://search.proquest.com/openview/cdc22487ae3db68935bf1d396839cabd/1?pq-origsite=gscholar&cbl=2026366&diss=y

Haruna, H. (2025). Decision-Making, AI Auditing: Establishing Governance and Compliance in Algorithmic. *Reinventsecurity.Org*.

Hiraltalsaniya. (2023). Anomaly Detection with Unsupervised Machine Learning. *Medium*. https://medium.com/simform-engineering/anomaly-detection-with-unsupervised-machine-learning-3bcf4c431aff

Kaur, R., Gabrijelčič, D., & Klobučar, T. (2023). Artificial intelligence for cybersecurity: Literature review and future research directions. *Information Fusion*, *97*, 101804. https://doi.org/10.1016/j.inffus.2023.101804

Loza, B. (2025). Reinforcement Machine Learning in Cybersecurity: A Comprehensive Analysis. *Medium*. https://medium.com/@leev574/reinforcement-machine-learning-in-cybersecurity-a-comprehensive-analysis-17c2505c8be0

Nvidia. (2025). *NetworkX*. https://www.nvidia.com/en-gb/glossary/networkx/

Security Patterns.io. (2024). *Step By Step Guide: How to Write a Security Pattern*. https://securitypatterns.io/docs/how-to-write-a-security-pattern/

Sergi, B. S., Esposito, M., & Goyal, S. (2019). Emerging trends and future directions of e-commerce in global business landscape. *World Review of Entrepreneurship, Management and Sustainable Development, 15*(1/2), 226. https://doi.org/10.1504/WREMSD.2019.10019882

Shrivastav, A., Chaturvedi, K., Sankathala, S., Patre, K., Saraf, A. H., & Das, S. (2025). *Artificial Intelligence (AI) in Cybersecurity* (pp. 29–56). https://doi.org/10.4018/979-8-3373-2252-0.ch002

About The Authors

Rahul Karne is a cybersecurity leader, digital forensics expert, and technology innovator, currently shaping enterprise defenses as a Security Analyst at American Airlines and as advisor to pioneering forensic startups. His career merges impactful work in threat detection, network automation, and digital investigations across large-scale enterprises and research settings. A CISSP-certified professional, Rahul has authored numerous academic publications and is recognized for his patents in cybersecurity. With a talent for deploying AI-driven solutions and architecting resilient cloud systems, he champions intelligent, secure technology for the next generation of digital enterprises, blending technical rigor with practical insight to solve real-world challenges.

Sai Teja Erukude builds AI that actually ships. A Data Scientist at Koch Ag & Energy Solutions, he works at the intersection of responsible AI and real-world deployment, turning complex models into secure, scalable systems that deliver measurable impact.

Sai holds an M.S. in Computer Science from Kansas State University and has 5+ years of experience building AI-powered software. His extensive research has resulted in 17+ publications and a patent pending, and he serves as a peer reviewer for top-tier journals. His writing is guided by a simple goal: make advanced AI understandable, usable, and worth trusting.

Suhasnadh Veluru is an ERP System Administrator at Owen Equipment Company, where he seamlessly manages data-centric operations within enterprise systems. Holding a Master's degree in Data Analytics from Kansas State University, Suhasnadh brings a robust foundation in data engineering, analytics, and systems integration. With over five years of professional experience in data-driven roles, he has cultivated deep expertise in data management, reporting, and ERP systems. Passionate about data, Suhasnadh specializes in transforming complex data sets into actionable insights, ensuring operational efficiency and strategic growth.

Viswa Chaitanya Marella is a Database Administrator at Centralia College supporting enterprise data systems in the higher education sector. He specializes in database administration, business intelligence, and automation, with expertise in SQL Server and Power BI. Viswa works extensively with ERP and Student Information Systems such as PeopleSoft and focuses on building reliable data warehouses and automated pipelines that improve performance and reporting accuracy. His work supports data-driven decision-making across academic and administrative operations, and he continues to explore intelligent data technologies to strengthen institutional data ecosystems.

www.ingramcontent.com/pod-product-compliance
Lightning Source LLC
LaVergne TN
LVHW022215200926
848481LV00006B/1976

* 9 7 9 8 9 0 3 9 2 1 6 3 8 *